Flutter and Dart Cookbook
Developing Full-Stack Applications for the Cloud

Richard Rose
Foreword by Majid Hajian

Beijing · Boston · Farnham · Sebastopol · Tokyo

Flutter and Dart Cookbook

by Richard Rose

Published by O'Reilly Media, Inc., 1005 Gravenstein Highway North, Sebastopol, CA 95472.

O'Reilly books may be purchased for educational, business, or sales promotional use. Online editions are also available for most titles (*https://oreilly.com*). For more information, contact our corporate/institutional sales department: 800-998-9938 or *corporate@oreilly.com*.

Acquisitions Editor: Suzanne McQuade
Development Editor: Jeff Bleiel
Production Editor: Jonathon Owen
Copyeditor: nSight Inc.
Proofreader: Arthur Johnson

Indexer: Potomac Indexing LLC
Interior Designer: David Futato
Cover Designer: Karen Montgomery
Illustrator: Kate Dullea

December 2022:   First Edition

Revision History for the First Edition
2022-12-14   First Release

See *https://www.oreilly.com/catalog/errata.csp?isbn=0636920635109* for release details.

978-1-098-11951-5

[LSI]

Table of Contents

Foreword

Every day I see people building amazing apps and creating great content with Flutter and Dart. Both Flutter and Dart help developers learn faster and pursue their dreams. When Rich Rose told me he was writing this book, I knew it would help thousands of developers.

This cookbook's practical, example-driven approach provides a fascinating way to learn Flutter and Dart. As an early adopter of Flutter and Dart, Rich has done a tremendous job of sharing numerous valuable tips and tricks. It's a great desk reference in which you'll find answers to many questions that you face in your daily work.

I'm happy to recommend this book, and I hope it helps you unlock the potential of the fantastic experience of building Flutter apps and working with the Dart language.

—Majid Hajian
Google Developer Expert for Flutter and Dart
and Head of Developer Relations at Invertase
Oslo, November 2022

Preface

Welcome to the *Flutter and Dart Cookbook*. If you haven't heard of Flutter, it's the multiplatform framework that is taking the development community by storm. Dart provides a rich software development kit (SDK) underpinning Flutter. Rather than having to learn multiple technologies, Flutter enables you to target Android, iOS, Linux, the web, and Windows from a single code base.

As someone who watches a lot of YouTube, I am always deeply impressed with the example applications created. Flutter and Dart have been instrumental in not only making me love coding again but also allowing me to meet some awesome Flutter community folks.

The Flutter community is pretty dope and continues to deliver high-quality content— shout-out to YouTubers and Google Developer communities dedicating time and effort to help people get a foothold in the software industry.

Whether you are a seasoned developer or are just getting started, Flutter makes development fun. It's very quick to learn and super powerful, allowing integration with powerful cloud-based solutions such as Firebase. Get started today and build an application for the next million users.

Who Should Read This Book

Whether or not you know Flutter and Dart, you have heard that irresistible call to go out and build something. Ignore the desire to procrastinate, and get started building the future. So how do you maintain motivation and get to the point you are able to deliver an application? Read this book. The beauty of learning Flutter and Dart is it has a very low barrier to entry.

Developing an application requires both skill and effort. There is a reason software engineers are paid a lot of money. Whether you have experience in multiple languages or have zero experience developing software, Flutter and Dart is a great starting point to creating stunning applications. From the first day, you can quickly become productive and produce beautiful applications with very little effort.

Building applications involves lots of moving pieces as well as integrating with external services. Learn the fundamentals of working with the Firebase suite and take your first steps with Cloud. Get started building games and then follow along to understand the building blocks for the Flame game engine.

Why I Wrote This Book

I was first introduced to Flutter when my wife started learning the language using a Flutter development course created by Google. The main thing that stood out to me was the speed at which applications were built and how nice they looked. The immediate productivity boost was impressive, and I was quickly hooked on building simple multiplatform apps.

When I was starting out learning this new technology, there were a number of things which were either not obvious or just difficult to remember. I would have loved to have this cookbook to sit beside me while working on that course. Now there are even more superb courses available online, but the lingering question still remains, How do you do x in Flutter? For some readers, this book will complement your existing knowledge as you undertake your journey to create applications. For others, it will represent that safety blanket that you can use to guide and support your journey as a Flutter developer.

Navigating This Book

Getting started with any language can present lots of uncertainty as you wonder where to start and what you need to know. While I really want you to read the book from cover to cover, realistically you will likely jump directly to the Flutter chapters. With that in mind, the book features broad categories to give you the opportunity to dip into the subject matter as required. The general categories are as follows:

- Chapters 1 and 2 provide a high-level introduction to the Dart language to help you work with the basics such as variables and control flow.
- Chapters 3 to 6 give you a rapid immersion into the essential elements of the Dart language that will help you use the language productively.
- Chapters 7 to 14 cover the Flutter language and demonstrate the basics of rendering widgets on-screen. If I had to guess, this is the section you will reference the most when developing applications that require widget creation and data management.
- Chapters 15 and 16 cover working in the cloud and specifically Firebase to add authentication, databases, and hosting.

- Chapter 17 deals with using the Flame game engine and gives you the essentials of this package. If you have a weekend free, you can use this to recreate the game Frogger.
- The Appendix covers the stuff that you need to know to set up your environment such as installing the Flutter framework, using Flutter Doctor, and working in an IDE.

Conventions Used in This Book

The following typographical conventions are used in this book:

Italic
: Indicates new terms, URLs, email addresses, filenames, and file extensions.

`Constant width`
: Used for program listings, as well as within paragraphs to refer to program elements such as variable or function names, databases, data types, environment variables, statements, and keywords.

`Constant width bold`
: Shows commands or other text that should be typed literally by the user.

`Constant width italic`
: Shows text that should be replaced with user-supplied values or by values determined by context.

 This element signifies a general note.

 This element signifies a general note.

O'Reilly Online Learning

O'REILLY® For more than 40 years, *O'Reilly Media* has provided technology and business training, knowledge, and insight to help companies succeed.

Our unique network of experts and innovators share their knowledge and expertise through books, articles, and our online learning platform. O'Reilly's online learning platform gives you on-demand access to live training courses, in-depth learning paths, interactive coding environments, and a vast collection of text and video from O'Reilly and 200+ other publishers. For more information, visit *https://oreilly.com*.

How to Contact Us

Please address comments and questions concerning this book to the publisher:

> O'Reilly Media, Inc.
> 1005 Gravenstein Highway North
> Sebastopol, CA 95472
> 800-998-9938 (in the United States or Canada)
> 707-829-0515 (international or local)
> 707-829-0104 (fax)

We have a web page for this book, where we list errata, examples, and any additional information. You can access this page at *https://oreil.ly/fl-dt-ckbk*.

Email *bookquestions@oreilly.com* to comment or ask technical questions about this book.

For news and information about our books and courses, visit *https://oreilly.com*.

Find us on LinkedIn: *https://linkedin.com/company/oreilly-media*

Follow us on Twitter: *https://twitter.com/oreillymedia*

Watch us on YouTube: *https://www.youtube.com/oreillymedia*

Acknowledgments

This edition is dedicated to my lovely wife, who inspired me to learn Flutter, only so she could get me to fix her applications. :-) Thanks to my family, who, despite Dad being busy writing this book, always made time to play music noisily or come and have an impromptu chat when I was deep in concentration. Seriously, though, thanks to Dawn, Bailey, Elliot, Noah, and Amelia. Over the course of a year, working on this book has become more than a project—it has become an inspiration.

Special thanks to Dylan Peck, Casey Palowitch, Alessandro Palmieri, and Andrew Brogdon for the support and the opportunity to deliver Flutter to the Google Developer Group community. It's acts like this that make the difference, and, from personal experience, know that these sessions are really appreciated.

I also want to thank the technical reviewers—Alex Moore, Rob Edwards, and Majid Hajian—for some great insight and feedback. While it's not easy writing a book, it is super helpful to have access to folks who are willing to dedicate their spare time and help deliver something like this. Really appreciate the effort and the time spent by each of you.

My deepest thanks to Jeff Bleiel for being a fantastic editor and someone who made this process very enjoyable and significantly less stressful than it should have been. Thanks also to Zan McQuade and Jonathon Owen at O'Reilly.

## CHAPTER 1

Learning Dart Variables

In this chapter, we focus on learning the basics of using variables in Dart. As you might expect, Dart offers a rich set of variable data types. To quickly get up to speed in the language, it is vitally important to know the basic data types.

If you are familiar with the use of variables in other programming languages, understanding variables in Dart should not be too difficult to grasp. Use this chapter as a quick guide to cement your understanding before moving on to more complex topics.

For beginners, this chapter will introduce you to the fundamentals. Ultimately it should offer a quick technical guide as you progress in your journey to learn Dart/Flutter.

Across the chapter, the code examples are self-contained and are focused on a typical use case. We start by discussing the four main variable types (i.e., `int`, `double`, `bool`, and `String`) and how each is used. Finally, we learn how to let Dart know what we want to do with our variables (i.e., `final`, `const`, and `null`).

We also cover the subject of immutability, which refers to the ability to change the value associated with a variable. An immutable variable is one that cannot be changed. In Dart, the keywords `const` and `final` make a variable immutable . A key nuance of immutability is whether the variable is checked at compile time or runtime. Compile time refers to checks applied at the code building stage (i.e., `const` variables). Runtime refers to checks performed at the application execution stage (i.e., `final` variables).

As of Dart 2.0, the language is type-safe, meaning that once a variable is declared, the type cannot be changed. For example, if a variable of type double is declared, it cannot then be used as an int without explicit casting. Before we dive into how to use variables, we need to ensure the programming environment is correctly set up.

1.1 Running a Dart Application

Problem

You want to run a dart application.

Solution

Dart code can be run within your environment once the SDK has been installed. To learn how to install the SDK, see the Appendix. Open a terminal session to allow the entry of commands. If you are using an IDE, the terminal needs to be opened within that application. Now confirm that Dart is installed on the device by checking the version as shown here:

```
dart --version
```

If the command responds successfully, you should see the version of the SDK installed and the platform you are running on. If the command is unsuccessful, you will need to check the installation and path for your device.

Now, in your editor, create a new file named *main.dart* and add the following contents:

```
void main() {
  print('Hello, Dart World!');
}
```

Run your example code from the command line as follows:

```
dart main.dart
```

This command should output "Hello, Dart World!"

Discussion

The `dart` command is available as part of the Dart SDK installation. In the preceding example, the command will run a file named *main.dart*. Dart applications have the extension *.dart* and can be run either from the command line or within an IDE (e.g., Android Studio or VS Code). Note: neither Android Studio nor VS Code are preconfigured to include Dart/Flutter functionality. You will need to install the relevant plug-in (in addition to installing the SDK) before being able to run any code.

If you don't want to install Dart within your environment, use the online editor available at DartPad (*https://dartpad.dev*).

If you are unable to run the `dart` command, it's likely that the SDK has not been installed correctly. Use the latest installation instructions (*https://dart.dev/get-dart*) to confirm the installation on your device.

1.2 Working with Integer Values

Problem

You want to store a number without a decimal point.

Solution

Use an integer variable to store a number without a decimal point.

If you want to store an integer value of 35, the declaration would be as follows:

```
void main() {
  int    myVariable = 35;

  print(myVariable);
}
```

In the Dart language, an integer uses the reference int. In the preceding code example, the data type (e.g., int) is the first part of the declaration. Next, a label is assigned to the data type to be used, e.g., myVariable. Finally, we assign a value to the data type—in this example, the value of 35.

To use the data type, a variable is declared, e.g., myVariable. A variable is a label used to reference the data type created.

Once a variable is available, you can assign a value to the data type. In the example, the integer 35 is assigned to the variable myVariable. A print statement is then used to output the variable value.

Discussion

Dart follows a set pattern for declaration of variables. The prefix declares the data type to be used; this is followed by a variable label and then an optional assignment.

In this example, the data type to be used is an int. An integer is represented by numbers that do not have a decimal point. The typical use case for an int is a number that doesn't require a decimal point (i.e., precision). An integer is defined as a 64-bit integer number. The integer data type is a subtype of num, which includes basic operations, e.g., +/–, etc.

The variable label provides a means to reference the int data type in the example code. Our example uses the label myVariable. When naming a variable, try to make the name relevant to the purpose of the variable.

To complete the variable declaration, a value is assigned. Here we assign the value of 35 to our variable, meaning when we reference this, we expect the value of 35 to be used for our int data type.

If the integer variable were not initialized, it would mean a value could not be accessed. In this situation, Dart will return an error indicating the value we are trying to access is a non-nullable variable. Essentially, this means we have not assigned a value to a variable we are attempting to access. In most instances, this is an error, and the Dart compiler will helpfully tell us we have made a mistake. If you do in fact wish to use a nullable variable, you would need to tell Dart how to handle this situation. Learn more about handling null values in Recipe 1.9.

1.3 Working with Double Values

Problem

You want to store a number with a decimal point.

Solution

Use a double (precision) variable to store a number including a decimal point.

If you want to store a double value of 2.99, declare the following:

```
void main() {
  double myVariable = 2.99;

  print(myVariable);
}
```

Similar to other variables, prefix the variable with the desired data type, e.g., double. The variable will then require a label to be assigned, e.g., myVariable. Finally, assign a value to the data type—in this example, the value of 2.99.

Discussion

In the previous example, we begin by indicating the data type to be used, i.e., double. Following that, we provide a variable name (in our example, myVariable) for double. The last part, where a value is assigned to the variable, is optional.

The typical use case for a double data type is a number requiring a level of precision. A double data type is a 64-bit floating-point number. Double is a subtype of num, which includes basic operations, e.g., +/−, etc.

1.4 Working with Boolean Values

Problem

You want to store a true/false value.

Solution

Use a `bool` variable to store a true/false state.

Declare a Boolean variable using the keyword `bool`, following the data type declaration with a label for the variable name, e.g., `myVariable`. Finally, assign a value to the variable of either `true` or `false`.

Here's an example of how to declare a `bool`:

```
void main() {
  bool myVariable = true;

  print(myVariable);
}
```

Discussion

In the preceding example, we begin by indicating the data type to be used, i.e., `bool`. Following that, we provide a variable name for the defined data type. The last part is optional, where we assign a value to the named variable.

The use case for a `bool` is that of a true/false scenario. Note that `true` and `false` are reserved keywords in Dart. *Reserved* in this context indicates the word has a defined meaning in terms of the language. A boolean data type includes logic operations, e.g., and, equality, inclusive or, exclusive or.

1.5 Working with Strings

Problem

You want to store a sequence of characters.

Solution

Use a `String` variable to store a series of text.

Here's an example of how to declare a `String`:

```
void main() {

  String myVariable  = "I am a string";

  String myVariable2  = """
    I am a multiline
    string
    """;

  print(myVariable);
}
```

Discussion

Begin by indicating the data type to be used, i.e., String. A string is used to represent a sequence of characters that can be both numbers and letters. Note that a String uses a capital for its data type, which is often the source of errors when first learning Dart.

The data type will require a variable for the defined data type, and this will be used to reference the associated value. An assignment of a value is optional at this stage.

The typical use case for a String data type is collection of text. A String data type in Dart uses 16-bit Unicode Transformation Format (UTF-16) code units. The String class is used to represent text characters but due to encoding can also support an extended range of characters, e.g., emojis.

When using a String variable, you can use either matching single or double quotes to identify the text to be displayed. If you require a multiline text, this can be achieved using triple quotes. In the example, you can see a demonstration of both of these types of declaration.

1.6 Printing Information to the Console

Problem

You want to display programmatic output from a Dart application.

Solution

Use a print statement to display information from an application. The print statement can display both static (i.e., a string literal) and variable content.

Here's an example of how to print static content:

```
void main() {

  print('Hello World!');
}
```

Here's an example of how to print the content of a variable:

```
void main() {

  int intVariable  = 10;
  var boolVariable = true;

  print(intVariable);
  print('$intVariable');
  print('The bool variable is $boolVariable');
}
```

Discussion

Use the $ character to reference a variable in a `print` statement. Prefixing a variable with the $ tells Dart that a variable is being used and it should replace this value.

The `print` statement is useful in a number of scenarios. Printing static content doesn't require any additional steps to display information. To use with static content, enclose the value in quotes and the `print` statement will take care of the rest.

Printing a variable value will require the variable to be prefixed with the $ sign. Where Dart is being used to print content, you can tell the language that you want the value to be displayed. In the second example, you see three common ways to reference a variable in a `print` statement.

Dart will provide feedback on whether a brace is required; typically it is not. However, if you create a complex variable type, do check to ensure you are referencing the element desired.

1.7 Adding a Constant Variable (Compile Time)

Problem

You want to create a variable that cannot be changed (immutable) at any point.

Solution

Use `const` to create a variable whose value cannot be reassigned and will be checked at compile time.

Here's an example of using a `const` variable:

```
void main() {
  const daysInYear = 365;

  print ('There are $daysInYear days in a year');
}
```

Discussion

In Dart, `const` represents a value that cannot be changed.

Use the `const` keyword where a variable is not subject to change. The example declares a `const` variable set to the number 365, meaning it is immutable across the scope of the application.

If you were to try to change the value within the application, you would see a compile time error indicating an assignment cannot be made due to the variable being designated as a const. Remove the comment associated with the line featuring days InYear = 10 to see this type of error.

The use of const is a good method to reduce errors within your application. Declaring variables as const provides a robust interface that uses the compiler to explicitly verify the use of variables.

1.8 Adding a Constant Variable (Runtime)

Problem

You want to create a variable that cannot be changed (immutable), but you will not know the value until the application is run (i.e., runtime).

Solution

Use final to create a variable whose value cannot be reassigned. In contrast to a const variable, a final variable value is assigned at runtime.

Here's an example using a final variable:

```
void main() {
  final today = DateTime.now();

  print('Today is day ${today.weekday}');
}
```

Discussion

Final represents a value that needs to be determined at runtime and is not subject to change. The final keyword is used in situations where a value is derived at runtime (i.e., when the application is active). Again, the value assigned is immutable; however, unlike a const value, it cannot be known at compile time.

If you attempt to perform an assignment to a final variable that has already been set, the compiler will generate an error.

In the code example, the day output by the print statement is returned by the Date Time function. The value returned is determined when the application is run, so it will display based on the actual weekday available on the host machine.

1.9 Working with Null Variables

Problem

You want to assign a variable a default value of null.

Solution

Use null to apply a consistent value to a declared variable. Null is an interesting concept, as it is meant to represent the absence of content. Typically a null value is used to initialize variables that do not have a default value to be assigned. In this instance null can be used to represent a variable that has not explicitly been assigned a value.

Here's an example of how to declare a variable as null in Dart:

```
void main(){
  int ?myVariable;
  print ('ten: $myVariable');

  myVariable = 10;
  print ('ten: $myVariable');
}
```

Discussion

To enable null to be assigned to a data type, it is expected that the ? type is appended to explicitly indicate a value can also be null. In the example, myVariable is set to nullable by prefixing the variable with ?.

In Dart, null is also an object, which means it can be used beyond the simple "no value" use case. More recent versions of the Dart SDK also require explicit acknowledgment of whether a data type is nullable or non-nullable.

Note that as of Dart v2.0, null type safety is now the default, meaning it is no longer possible to assign null to all data types.

For further information, consult the Null class reference in the Dart API (*https://oreil.ly/5TfdW*).

## CHAPTER 2

Exploring Control Flow

Control flow relates to the way instructions will be executed in an application. Typical logic flows exist, such as conditional and looping flows used to determine the instructional processing order. Dart provides a number of methods to manage how the application operates and coordinates based on this decision flow.

If you have used other languages such as Python, JavaScript, etc., then you will be very familiar with the content covered in this chapter. For those of you who are new to development, this chapter is super important! Control flow statements are common across most languages you will be exposed to. Part of learning a language is the ability to incorporate these types of statements.

In this chapter, you will learn how to use control flow to incorporate logic in your application. You'll also see use cases for each statement. Many of the flows include a condition statement that is used to dictate what actions are taken. Pay special attention to these conditions and look to efficiently use control flow within your application.

2.1 Verifying That a Condition Has Been Met

Problem

You want to provide a logical check on a condition before executing an instruction.

Solution

Use an `if` statement to provide a control statement for a binary option. An `if` statement provides a step to confirm that a logic statement is valid.

If there are multiple options, consider using a `switch` statement. (Reference Recipe 2.4)

This example shows how to use the `if` condition. The `if` statement is used to check the value of a `bool` variable. If the `bool` variable is set to `true`, then the first message is displayed. If the `bool` variable is set to `false`, an alternative message is displayed:

```
void main() {

  bool isFootball = true;

  if (isFootball) {
    print('Go Football!');
  } else {
    print('Go Sports!');
  }
}
```

Discussion

Working with an `if` statement allows control over the logic progression within an application. Control flow of this type is essential to building applications and provides a simple mechanism to select between choices. An `if` statement conditional flow is outlined in Figure 2-1.

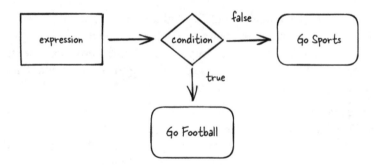

Figure 2-1. *If statement control logic*

In the example, the `if` statement validation is implicit, meaning it is checking that the value assigned is `true`. Logical operators such as && (AND) and || (OR) can also be used to extend the expressions to be tested. Use the AND operator to validate that both expressions are `true` before executing the code. A logical OR is used to assert if one or more of the expressions is `true`, where each expression is evaluated in turn. Additionally, the logical operators can be reversed with the use of the ! (invert) operator on a Boolean value.

The typical use case for an `if` statement is to make a choice between two or more options. If you have only two options, this type of control flow is ideal.

In addition to the preceding, a *"collection if"* provides additional functionality to test an element. The data associated with the element can be set based on the collection object condition, e.g., whether it is the first or last object in a data structure.

2.2 Iterating Until a Condition Is Met

Problem

You want a method to loop until a condition is satisfied within an application.

Solution

Use a while loop when you need the entry condition to be validated at the start of the control flow. Note: the loop check is performed at the start of the loop condition. A while loop therefore has a minimum of zero iterations and a max iteration of *N*.

Here's an example of a while loop control flow:

```
void main() {

  bool isTrue = true;

  while (isTrue) {
    print ('Hello');
    isTrue = false;
  }
}
```

Use a do while loop when you need the loop to be executed a minimum of one iteration.

As you can see in Figure 2-2, the loop condition is checked on entry, meaning this loop construct will be validated before each iteration.

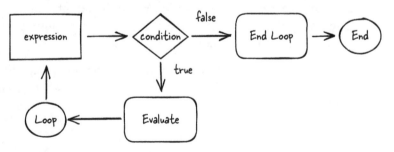

Figure 2-2. While loop logic

Here's an example of a control flow do while loop:

```
void main() {

  bool isTrue = true;

  do {
    print ('Hello');
    isTrue = false;
  } while (isTrue) ;
}
```

In contrast, notice how the loop shown in Figure 2-3 varies from the previous example of a while condition.

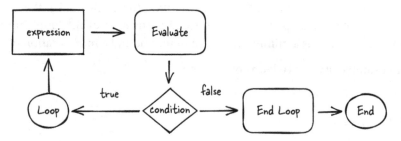

Figure 2-3. Do while loop

With this control structure, the condition is validated at the end of the statements, meaning the loop will execute at least once.

Discussion

The key nuance to observe from these examples is the nature of execution and what that means for processing of the control flow.

In the while loop example, the demo application will only output a value when the bool variable is set to true. The do while loop example will output a print statement irrespective of the initial value of the isTrue variable.

A while loop will test a condition before executing the loop, meaning you can use this to perform 0...N iterations. A typical use case would be one where a variable is used to control the number of iterations performed.

In a do while statement, the typical use case would be one where there is at least a single loop iteration. If the situation requires a single iteration, then using this type of control flow is a good choice.

2.3 Iterating over a Range of Items

Problem

You want a method to loop through a defined range of items.

Solution

Use a for statement to perform a defined number of iterations within a defined range. The specific range is determined as part of the initialization of the for statement.

Here's an example of a for statement:

```
void main() {

  int maxIterations = 10;
  for (var i = 0; i < maxIterations; i++) {
    print ('Iteration: $i');
  }
}
```

In addition, where you have objects accessible using a loop (i.e., iterable), you can also use forEach:

```
void main() {
  List daysOfWeek = ['Sunday', 'Monday', 'Tuesday'];

  daysOfWeek.forEach((print));
}
```

Discussion

A for statement can be used for a variety of use cases, such as performing an action an exact number of times (e.g., initializing variables).

In Figure 2-4, the for loop is used to iterate over items. Similar to a while loop, the condition is checked on entry, and if it is met, the loop exits. If the condition is not met, the loop continues until the range of items has been exhausted.

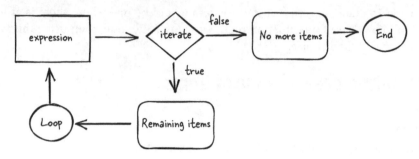

Figure 2-4. For loop

As the second example shows, a `forEach` statement is a very useful technique to access information within an object. Where you have an iterable type (e.g., the `List` object), a `forEach` statement provides the ability to directly access the content. Appending the `forEach` to the `List` object enables a shortcut in which a `print` statement can be directly attributed to each item in the list.

The typical use case for a `for` statement is to perform iterations where a range is defined. It can also be used to efficiently process a `List` or similar data type in an efficient manner.

2.4 Performing Conditional Actions Based on a Value

Problem

You want to perform multiple logical checks on a presented value.

Solution

Use a `switch` statement where you have multiple logic statements. Typically, where multiple logical checks are required, the first control flow to come to mind might be an `if` statement (which we saw in Recipe 2.1). However, it may be more efficient to use a `switch` statement.

Here's an example of a `switch` statement:

```
void main() {
  int myValue = 2;

  switch (myValue) {
    case 1: print('Monday');
      break;
    case 2: print('Tuesday');
      break;
    default:
```

```
        print('Error: Value not defined?');
        break;
    }
}
```

Discussion

A `switch` (or `case`) statement provides an improved `if` statement for handling multiple conditions. In Figure 2-5, the `case` statement operates in the same way as an `if` statement, only there are multiple conditions to be checked. For most purposes, a `case` statement represents a more readable `if` condition for situations where two or more conditions are to be validated.

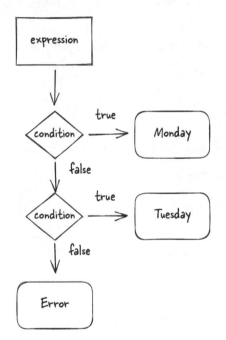

Figure 2-5. Switch statement

In Figure 2-5, observe how multiple conditions are available. A `switch` statement can present better readability over multiple `if` statements. In most cases where the requirements need a logical condition to be validated, the `switch` statement may offer a stylistically cleaner choice.

In the example code, the `switch` statement has two valid choices, i.e., 1 or 2. Hopefully you can imagine expanding this code to incorporate more choices.

The `switch` statement will render the default statement where the relevant value has not been added. That is, any other choice is sent to the default option, which acts as a cleanup section. Incorporating explicit statements is helpful to reduce errors in processing of information.

2.5 Using an Enumerator to Represent Values

Problem

You want to define a grouping of constant values to use within an application.

Solution

Use an enum (enumeration) to provide a grouping of information that is a consistent model for associated data.

Here's an example of declaring and printing the values associated with the enum:

```
enum Day { sun, mon, tues }

void main() {
  print(Day.values);
}
```

Here's an example of declaring and printing the enum reference at index zero:

```
enum Day { sun, mon, tues }

void main() {
  print('${Day.values[0]}');
}
```

Here's an example of using the values.byName:

```
enum Day { sun, mon, tues }

void main() {
  print(Day.values.byName('mon'));
}
```

Discussion

The preceding examples demonstrate the versatility of enums when writing code in Dart. At the time of writing, Dart only supports enum definitions at the top level of scope, meaning you can't move the definition inside a class or a function.

An enum (or enumeration) is used to define related items. Think of an enum as an ordered collection—for example, days of the week or months of the year. In the examples, the order can be transposed with the value, e.g., the first month is January or the twelfth month is December.

In the first example, you see how the enum can be used to output a series of values. Generally an enum can simplify overall data access. If a specific element within an enum is required, this can also be achieved, as shown in the second example.

In the third example, rather than access an enum value by a numerical index, Dart has added a byName method. The method enables you to use the name associated with the enum value for easier data access. When the print command is run, the debug output shows the values associated with the enum, i.e., "mon." Enum is still indexed; however, you can now use a more convenient method to access each item rather than a numerical value based on its position.

2.6 Implementing Exception Handling

Problem

You want to provide a way to handle error processing within an application.

Solution

Use the try, catch, and finally blocks to provide exception management in Dart.

Here's an example of how to handle exceptions in Dart:

```
void main(){
  String name = "Dart";

  try{
    print ('Name: $name');
    // The following line generates a RangeError
    name.indexOf(name[0], name.length - (name.length+2));
  } on RangeError catch (exception) {
    print ('On Exception: $exception');
  }
  catch (exception) {
    print ('Catch Exception: $exception');
  } finally {
    print ('Mission completed!');
  }
}
```

Discussion

The example code defines the relevant sections and sets up a String to hold the word "Dart."

In Figure 2-6 we have a String variable allocation based on four memory slots. To generate an exception, the indexOf method is used with an invalid range (i.e., one greater than the length of the String variable). Moving beyond the last item in the

`String` allocated memory will generate a `RangeError` exception. The exception explicitly indicates the error it is seeing, so in the example, the range provided for the index is invalid for the variable declared.

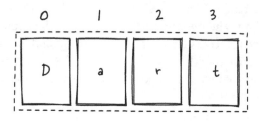

Figure 2-6. Exception handling example

A `try` block is used for normal processing of code. The block of code will continue executing until an event indicates something abnormal is occurring. Typically you will place your code in a `try` block to capture exceptions.

An on block is used to handle a specific type of exception being raised. In the example, the `RangeError` is anticipated to occur. If you want to handle a specific exception type being generated, use the on keyword in your exception block.

A `catch` block is used to handle general processing where an abnormal event occurs. Using a `catch` block provides an opportunity to safely recover or handle the event that took place. In most situations, you may not be able to identify the type of exception being generated prior to the event. Use the `catch` block to allow your code to react in a graceful manner when an error occurs.

A `finally` block is used to perform an action that should take place irrespective of whether code is successfully executed or generates an exception. Typically, a `finally` block is used for cleanup, e.g., to close any open files, etc. In addition, it will output a message to indicate the processing has been completed irrespective of the exception occurring.

Exception management is certainly a type of control flow, although not in the traditional sense. Adding exception management will become ever more important to your application as it increases in complexity.

## CHAPTER 3

Implementing Functions

In this chapter, we will move beyond the fundamentals of Dart and introduce functions. As you may have noticed, we have already used a number of functions (e.g., `main` and `print`). In this chapter we will explore the main use cases for using functions.

Building more complex applications will certainly require developers to progress beyond simple constructs. At a minimum, an awareness of some essential concepts and algorithms is desirable. Over the course of this chapter you will learn the foundations of code isolation.

The main use case for functions is to group instructions. The chapter begins by illustrating how to define a basic function without parameters or a return value. In most situations, this is not the pattern you will want to use. However, for learning purposes it has been included. Beyond this you will be introduced to parameters and return values. At this point, hopefully it will become clearer why adding parameters and return values is so powerful and the desired pattern to follow.

Toward the end of the chapter you will see examples of other ways to use functions. You'll discover that, as your skills grow as a developer, so will your use of functions.

3.1 Declaring Functions

Problem

You want a common group name for instructions that perform a specific task.

Solution

Declare a function to consolidate the instructions for a task. In the following example, the getCurrentDateTime function is used to print out a date/time value:

```
void main() {
  getCurrentDateTime();
}

void getCurrentDateTime() {
  var timeLondon  = DateTime.now();
  print('London:    $timeLondon');
}
```

Discussion

Dart uses the main() function as the starting point for an application. The boilerplate code takes no arguments and expects no return value (i.e., void). From this function, we can both create and call other functions to handle the processing within our application.

In the preceding example we create a utility function named getCurrentDateTime. Note that the function is declared as requiring no parameters, and a void return similar to the main function. The role of the getCurrentDateTime function is to grab the current DateTime. To do this it calls a library function named DateTime.now(), which returns the current time when run.

While you could add the code directly into the main function, we now have a way to access the current date, which can easily be added to other programs. As we have grouped the functionality in a separate function, this can be isolated and used as required in other programs. Establishing functional isolation within your programs is a good habit to acquire and means you will likely be able to reuse more of your code as time goes on.

3.2 Adding Parameters to Functions

Problem

You want to pass variable information to a function.

Solution

Use a parameter to pass information to a function. In the following example, a parameter is provided to a function as used as part of the control flow.

```
void main() {
  getCurrentDateTime(-7);
}

void getCurrentDateTime(int hourDifference) {
  var timeNow  = DateTime.now();
  var timeDifference = timeNow.add(Duration(hours: hourDifference));

  print('The time now is:  $timeNow');
  print('The time minus 7 hours is:  $timeDifference');
}
```

Discussion

In the preceding example, the parameter provided to the function is used to determine an action. The function is used to determine a specific hour difference using the current time as returned by `DateTime.now()`.

Given we have added a parameter value to the function, we can now state the number of hours difference required. Doing this has made the function more applicable to a wider series of use cases. However, because the function doesn't return the value, the function isn't as flexible as it could be.

Using parameters enhances the flexibility of a function by adding a variable. The addition of variables to the function signature makes the function more general in nature. Creating generalized functions in this way is a good approach to reduce the amount of code that needs to be created for a task.

3.3 Using Optional Parameters

Problem

You want to vary the number of parameters to a function.

Solution

Provide an optional parameter. Dart supports optional parameters that enable values to be omitted. Two distinct types of optional parameters are available: named and positional.

Here's an example of how to use named parameters:

```
void main() {
  printGreetingNamed();
  printGreetingNamed(personName: "Rich");
  printGreetingNamed(personName: "Mary", clientId: 001);
}
```

```dart
void printGreetingNamed({String personName = 'Stranger',
                         int clientId = 999}){
  if (personName.contains('Stranger')) {
    print('Employee: $clientId Stranger danger ');
  } else {
    print('Employee: $clientId $personName ');
  }
}
```

Here's an example of how to use positional parameters:

```dart
void main() {
  printGreetingPositional("Rich");
  printGreetingPositional("Rich", "Rose");
}

void printGreetingPositional(String personName, [String? personSurname]){
  print(personName);
  if (personSurname != null){
    print(personSurname);
  }
}
```

Discussion

Dart provides additional flexibility for the use of parameters to functions. Where parameters can be omitted, it can be useful to consider the use of optional parameters.

Named parameters provide the ability to include named variables within the function declaration. To use this type of parameter, include braces to define the necessary values to be presented. In the first example, optional parameters are used to pass across a name and clientId. If the function is not supplied with the information, it will still operate as expected by defaulting to a value. Default values can be supplied if it is necessary to provide a value and perform specific logic, e.g., "int clientId = 999."

Positional parameters perform similarly to normal parameters, with the flexibility to be omitted as necessary. In the second example, the second parameter is defined as a positional parameter using the square brackets. Additionally, Dart allows the variable to be defined as a potentially null value by the inclusion of the ? character.

Both named and positional parameters offer increased flexibility to your functions. You can use them in a variety of scenarios where parameters are needed (for example, in a person object where first name and surname are mandatory, but the middle name is optional).

3.4 Returning Values from Functions

Problem

You want a common group name for instructions that return a computed value.

Solution

Use a named function that computes a value and returns this to the calling method. This is a common mechanism for grouping instructions together.

Here's an example of declaring a function that returns a value:

```
void main() {
  DateTime timeNow  = getCurrentDateTime(0);
  DateTime timeDifference = getCurrentDateTime(-7);

  print('The time now is:  $timeNow');
  print('The time minus 7 hours is:  $timeDifference');
}

DateTime getCurrentDateTime(int hourDifference) {
  DateTime timeNow  = DateTime.now();
  DateTime timeDifference = timeNow.add(Duration(hours: hourDifference));

  return timeDifference;
}
```

Discussion

In the preceding example, the function named `getCurrentDateTime` is enhanced to return a value. The function is declared to accept parameters and return a value. Now we have a more generic function that can be utilized in a wider series of settings.

In this instance, the function accepting parameters means you are able to provide different hour values. The function only knows that it should accept an `int` value representing the number of hours to be used. From the example we see we make two calls to the function, to initialize the current time with a zero hours difference, followed by a time difference with negative 7 hours.

The return value from the `getCurrentDateTime` function presents a `DateTime` object. By capturing the return value, you can output the relative date-time combination.

Note how we have reused the function to be invoked with an integer parameter and then return a `DateTime` object. Dart provides the opportunity to create simple functionality like this to help with your development. Having a rich set of methods associated with the class objects like `DateTime` saves an enormous amount of development time.

3.5 Declaring Anonymous Functions

Problem

You want to enclose an expression within a function.

Solution

Declare an anonymous function to perform a simple expression. Often a function only requires a single expression, in which case an anonymous function can provide an elegant solution.

Here's an example of how to use an anonymous function:

```
void main() {
  int value = 5;

  // Anonymous Function - Style 1
  int ex1Squared(num1) => num1 * num1;
  int ex1Cubed(num1)   => num1 * num1 * num1;

  // Anonymous Function - Style 2
  int ex2Squared(num1){ return num1 * num1; }
  int ex2Cubed(num1){ return num1 * num1 * num1; }

  print('EX1: $value squared is ${ex1Squared(value)}');
  print('EX1: $value cubed is ${ex1Cubed(value)}');

  print('EX2: $value squared is ${ex2Squared(value)}');
  print('EX2: $value cubed is ${ex2Cubed(value)}');
}
```

Discussion

In the example, a function has been created to square/cube a number as required. The algorithm takes an input and multiplies it, returning the result to the caller. You will note that the functions don't include a name and are anonymous. Typically you will see anonymous functions used for short pieces of code that are used to return a value. Prior to the function, a variable is declared to hold the result from the function. Note: the variable can include parameters by adding these within the bracket declaration.

Anonymous functions will typically use the => to indicate a function. In the example, the first functions declared use this style. The function return is implicit in this type of declaration, meaning you will have access to the result of the expression performed.

The second style outline performs the same task; however, note that an explicit return is used to provide access to the result. Stylistically, the choice is down to you as the developer as to which one is preferred.

Dart enables first-class functions, which essentially means they can be used in conjunction with a function (passed as arguments) and data structures. In the example, notice how the print statement is able to process the embedded functions to retrieve the result. Another use case would be as part of a forEach loop that makes a function call per iteration.

3.6 Adding a Functional Delay Using a Future

Problem

You want to introduce a custom delay that will await a completion state.

Solution

Use a Future to perform a specified programmatic delay in your code. Here's an example of how to use a Future to achieve a programmatic delay:

```
void main() async {
  int myDelay = 5;

  print ('Hello');

  var value = await _customDelay(myDelay);
  var customText = myDelay == 1 ? "second later": "seconds later";

  print ('Its $value $customText');
}

Future <int> _customDelay(int delay) async {
  try {
    await Future.delayed(Duration(seconds: delay));
    return delay;
  } catch (e) {
    print(e);
    return delay;
  }
}
```

Discussion

In the example, the code will implement a custom delay based on the number specified in the main function. A call to _customDelay uses a Future, which is an asynchronous operation featuring two states (e.g., completed and uncompleted). Asynchronous operations are typically used to wait for another operation to finish. In this example, we want to delay the program before printing out the final message indicating how long of a delay has been used.

The `Future` class is used in a number of situations, typically for loading longer-running processes that may need a bit of time to complete. In Chapter 13, the `Future` class will be used specifically with remote data access.

When using a `Future`, you will see two specific things that denote its inner workings. The first is the reference to `async`, which indicates an asynchronous function is being used. In addition, you may see a reference to the `await` keyword, meaning "at this point please wait for a response before continuing." The code will then await the completed state for the asynchronous expression.

## CHAPTER 4

Handling Lists and Maps

In this chapter, the fundamentals of data handling with Dart are outlined. The aim of this chapter is to cover Lists and Maps that are used to provide foundational data structures for information handling in Dart.

If you are lucky enough to be familiar with other languages, then many of the concepts presented should be familiar. However, in case this is your first time seeing these techniques, the example pieces of code are self-contained. You may find it helpful to run and experiment with the examples to gain a feel of the workings of the language.

The chapter begins by discussing Lists, which are indexable data structures used to hold objects. Lists are very common elements in Dart, as they can be used in a variety of scenarios.

We also discuss how to use Maps, which are useful for handling key/value pairs. A key/value pair is an associative relationship where the key is used as an index to access a value. For example, you may have a months of the year data structure in which the key is a number and the value is derived from the number, e.g., 1 generates the month January and 12 denotes December.

Over the course of this chapter, you will learn how to utilize Maps and Lists within your application.

4.1 Creating Lists of Data

Problem

You want a way to use a list of values within a Dart application.

Solution

Use a List to organize objects as an ordered collection. A List represents an array object that can hold information. It provides a simple construct that uses a zero-indexed grouping of elements.

Here's an example of how to use a List in Dart:

```
void main() {
  List listMonths = ['January', 'February', 'March'];

  listMonths.forEach(print);
}
```

Discussion

Lists are very versatile and can be used in a variety of circumstances. In the preceding example, a List class is used to hold the months of the year, as shown in Figure 4-1.

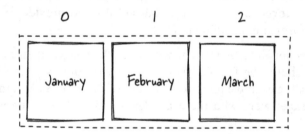

Figure 4-1. List data structure

The List declaration is used to hold a String, but it can actually hold a variety of data types, making this object extremely flexible. The List class provides a number of helpful methods such as forEach, length, reverse, isEmpty, and isNotEmpty. Each element within the List is directly addressable as well as being capable of being accessed via a forEach method.

A List is denoted by the use of square start and end brackets. Within the square brackets are the List elements, separated by commas. List items can be initialized at declaration or amended at a later time during processing.

The length of the List is available as a method, and this is used to identify how many elements are currently available. Note the List is indexed from zero, so if you intend to manually access elements, you will need to use zero if you want the first element.

Another nice feature of Lists is that they include a range of methods to handle processing information. In the example, the forEach method is used to perform a print of the elements contained in the List.

As you become more confident with Dart, Lists will become one of the many tools that are essential in the applications you write.

4.2 Amending a List of Data

Problem

You want to add new content to an existing List.

Solution

Use the List `add` method to incorporate new content into a List. Lists support the dynamic addition of new elements and can be expanded as required.

Here's an example of how to add a List element in Dart:

```
void main() {
  List listMonths = ['January', 'February', 'March'];

  listMonths.add('April');

  listMonths.forEach(print);
}
```

Discussion

In the preceding example code, a List is initially defined with three elements. If you want to expand the number of elements, this can be done by using the List `add` method. The add method will append the new element at the end of the List.

When you append a new element, as in Figure 4-2, the `List` class takes care of all the associated processing. The method `add` knows how to append the information passed and will ensure the relevant class properties (e.g., `length`) are updated. Therefore, in the example, you would see the months output as "January," "February," "March," "April." You will also see that the length of the List is amended to reflect that a fourth item has been added.

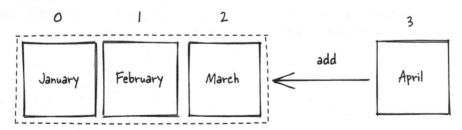

Figure 4-2. Adding an item to a List

The dynamic nature of a List makes it perfect for multiple situations where data structure manipulation is required. You will see Lists used across a number of situations to handle a variety of data types.

4.3 Using Lists with Complex Types

Problem

You want to make a List based on a combination of Strings and integers to create a new complex data type.

Solution

Use Lists to organize the consolidation of other data types. Lists can be especially useful for handling other data structures such as Maps (see Recipe 4.4).

Here's an example of how to use a List with complex data types in Dart:

```
void main() {
  Map<String, dynamic> filmStarWars = {"title": "Star Wars",
                                        "year": 1977};
  Map<String, dynamic> filmEmpire   = {"title": "The Empire Strikes Back",
                                        "year": 1980};
  Map<String, dynamic> filmJedi     = {"title": "The Return of the Jedi",
                                        "year": 1983};

  List listFilms = [filmStarWars, filmEmpire, filmJedi];

  Map<String, dynamic> currentFilm = listFilms[0];

  print(currentFilm);
  print(currentFilm['title']);
}
```

Discussion

In the example, film data is added to a Map that encloses title and year information, as shown in Figure 4-3. Here we use a List to manage the individual Maps, so the individual elements can be combined. The resultant List provides a convenient data structure for accessing the information to be stored.

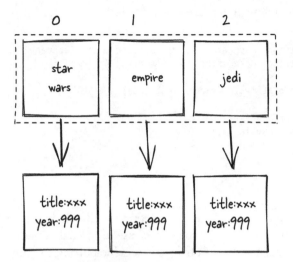

Figure 4-3. List with complex data type

Accessing the information within the List follows the same process as a normal List. To access the information, you need to dereference the variable. In this context, to dereference, use an index to tell Dart that you want to access the property value. The `listFilms[0]` means to access the first element in the List.

Once you have access to the List, the data type can then be accessed based on the associated data type. The example code uses a Map to allocate multiple values together. As each element is a Map, you now have the data associated with this. Use the dereferenced value to store in a new variable `currentFilm`, which can be accessed directly or with a key.

Using Lists can provide an elegant method to access complex data types in a consistent manner. If you need to coordinate data types, consider using a List to make this process more manageable.

4.4 Handling Map Key/Value Pairings

Problem

You want to handle a key/value pair in a Dart application.

Solution

Use a Map to handle key/value objects of any type. Map keys are required to be unique, as they act as the index to access Map values. Map values are not required to be unique and can be duplicated as needed.

Here's an example of how to declare a Map in Dart:

```
void main() {
  Map<int, String> mapMonths  = {0: 'January', 1: 'February', 2: 'March'};
  Map<int, String> moreMonths = {3: 'April', 4: 'May'};

  mapMonths.addEntries(moreMonths.entries);

  mapMonths.forEach((key, value){
    print('$key: $value');
  });
}
```

Discussion

In the code example, a Map is used to define a collection of data based on month information. A construct of this type is very useful to enable pieces of information to be combined together that benefit from a key/value pairing, as shown in Figure 4-4.

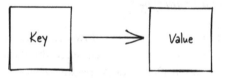

Figure 4-4. Map data structure

The month Map structure builds a relationship between the key and the value, e.g., Month 0 is January and January is Month 0. The structure of a Map is very useful in terms of processing list information, such as JavaScript Object Notation (JSON).

Declaration of the Map follows a standard variable format. Note: Map is actually a function call, so this requires the addition of braces. In our example, we indicate that the Map will be composed of an integer and a string, which means a number is used for the key (i.e., index). The string value field holds the reference to the month. You could also define the value as dynamic, which would allow the use of different variable types, providing additional flexibility. To be more specific, you could introduce the dynamic definition to explicitly replace the string. If you make this change, Dart will automatically infer the correct data type based on the variable assignment.

To populate the Map, define a key (e.g., mapMonth) and then assign a value (e.g., January). The assignment of values can be made in any order; the important thing is to be careful not to duplicate the keys used.

Adding an element to the Map requires both a key and a value. In the example, an additional Map structure called aprilMonth is created. Add the new month to the existing structure by calling the addEntries method with the parameter of the new Month Map.

To access the information within the Map class, use the Map methods and properties. A Map has a number of methods available that can be used to access the associated data items. To loop through each item, use the key to access the individual items. The example uses the Map `forEach` method to access each data structure item. With access to the key, the information associated with the Map can be retrieved by combining these elements together.

Regarding access to data, it is always worth checking the style guide information provided by the Dart team. In this instance, rather than use a `forEach`, you could also use a `for` loop. The guidance associated with access is defined in the Dart documentation (*https://oreil.ly/hRU0_*).

As the Dart language matures and guidelines are changed, it is good to be able to understand the reasoning behind them. The general tip to you the developer is to keep an awareness of these changes and look to respond to general guidance to avoid more complex refactoring in later development stages.

4.5 Printing Map Data Structure Content

Problem

You want to output the value of a Map data variable.

Solution

Use a Map to reference an indexed item. Map values are referenced as key/value combinations, which can be assigned to a variable for easier access.

Here's an example of retrieving a Map property and outputting the value with Dart:

```
void main() {
  Map<int, String> mapMonths = {0: 'January', 1: 'February', 2: 'March'};

  print ("Month: ${mapMonths[0]}");
  print ("Map: $mapMonths");
}
```

Discussion

In the code example, the value within the Map structure is accessed via its integer key. When a value is required, we provide the key to index the Map and retrieve the desired value. The first `print` statement explicitly requests the information associated with the key [0]. The use of braces around the variable is required to ensure we output the value of the month. In the second `print` statement, we output the entire Map for the `mapMonths` variable.

If you don't want to create individual variables to hold the values, remember to deference the Map values. In the print statement the braces are added to indicate to the Dart compiler we want the variable values rather than the contents of the Map.

4.6 Validating That Content Exists in a Map

Problem

You want to confirm that a key exists in a Map.

Solution

Use the indexing functionality of a Map to identify if a key explicitly exists.

Here's an example of validating that a key exists in a Map with Dart:

```
void main() {
  Map<int, String> mapMonths = {0: 'January', 1: 'February', 2: 'March'};

  if (mapMonths[0]!=null) {
    print ('Test 1: Key exists');
  }

  if (mapMonths.containsKey(2)) {
    print('Test 2: Key exists');
  }
}
```

Discussion

Maps are indexed using key values, so validating the existence of a key can quickly be performed. To find a key, use the required key to index the Map.

In the example, the Map will return a null value where the key is not present in the Map. An explicit check can be performed to ascertain if the value exists by checking for a non-null return. An alternative check would be to use the containsKey method to verify the value exists. From a functional perspective, the if statements are performing the same check.

Stylistically, you may prefer one approach over another. If the key exists in the Map, the information returned will be the value associated with the key.

4.7 Printing Complex Data Types

Problem

You want to output a variable based on a complex data type.

Solution

Use a `print` statement to display information from an application. The `print` statement will need to be formatted to correctly interpolate the data type to be displayed.

Here's an example of a how to print the complex data type:

```dart
import 'dart:convert';

void main() {
  // Create JSON value
  Map<String, dynamic> data = {
    jsonEncode('title'): json.encode('Star Wars'),
    jsonEncode('year'): json.encode(1977)
  };

  // Decode the JSON
  Map<String, dynamic>  items = json.decode(data.toString());

  print(items);
  print(items['title']);
  print("This is the title: $items['title']");
  print('This is the title: ${items['title']}');
}
```

Discussion

Use the $ character to reference a variable in a `print` statement. Prefixing a variable with the $ tells Dart that a variable is being used and it should replace this value.

The following examples from the last two `print` statements illustrate use cases that you will come across where the variable value needs a bit of help to be displayed correctly.

In the first use case, there is `String` interpolation without braces:

```dart
print("This is the title: $items['title']");
```

In the second use case, there is `String` interpolation with braces:

```dart
print('This is the title: ${items['title']}');
```

The preceding statements look equivalent, but they are not. In the first `print` statement, Dart will interpret the variable to be displayed as items. To display the variable correctly, it actually requires that it be enclosed in braces, as per the second line. Doing this will ensure that the value associated with `items['title']` is correctly interpreted by the `print` statement.

## CHAPTER 5

Getting Started with Object-Oriented Dart

In this section we introduce object-oriented techniques for working with classes and demonstrate how these can be used together with Dart. Over the course of the chapter you will explore both declaration and extension of objects. These techniques are important, as Dart is an object-oriented language. Learning the basics will provide a good reference to increase your own skill levels and incorporate other people's code more easily.

The chapter begins with a brief overview of the key terminology associated with object-oriented programming in relation to Dart. We then discuss how to incorporate a class into your programming repertoire. In addition, we also cover:

- The basics of object-oriented programming
- The need for class initialization through constructors
- Supporting inheritance through the `extends` keyword
- Defining a class signature by using an interface
- Aggregating class functionality with a mixin

As your development becomes more sophisticated, you will be able to utilize custom classes to achieve your requirements. Becoming efficient with classes has a steep learning curve, so take small steps. Over time, you will naturally improve and be able to incorporate very complex subject matter into your general solutions.

5.1 Beginning Object-Oriented Dart

Problem

You want to use object-oriented programming with Dart to build reusable components.

Solution

Use object-oriented techniques with Dart to develop code reflecting the composable objects that reflect the objective being modeled. Dart supports object-oriented techniques and encourages their use when developing algorithms and data structures needed to create your applications.

Discussion

Building your knowledge of object-oriented development will dramatically improve your skill set in Dart and Flutter. Learning how to create objects is a foundation skill and will help to build your understanding of how to link algorithms with data structures. Typically, an object will need to be initialized via a special method called a constructor. A constructor is responsible for setting the properties within the object during the initialization phase.

An object reflects the grouping of code and data types into a representative structure. For example, a book class and the initialized (instantiated) object may have a `title`, `author`, and `publisher` as properties.

In Figure 5-1, the book class provides the definition, and the book object is the runtime version of the class. The book class may also have other properties (e.g., `isbn`) or methods to retrieve (get) and update (set) the associated properties. The convenience of group data and code together in a class definition will become more familiar to you as you use the Dart language.

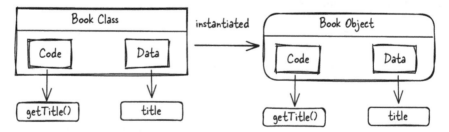

Figure 5-1. Book class example

To get started with object-oriented programming in Dart, learn the use cases for inheritance (see Recipe 5.4), implementation (see Recipe 5.5), and extending (see Recipe 5.6) to enable you to select the most appropriate design pattern for your implementation scenarios.

5.2 Creating a Class

Problem

You want to create a class object that represents both data and functionality.

Solution

Use a class to collate information into a new object providing both variable storage and functionality to process information. Here's an example of how to declare a class in Dart:

```
const numDays = 7;

class DaysLeftInWeek {
  int currentDay = 0;

  DaysLeftInWeek(){
    currentDay = DateTime.now().weekday.toInt();
  }

  int howManyDaysLeft(){
    return numDays - currentDay;
  }
}
```

Discussion

Dart is an object-oriented language and has the Object class (*https://oreil.ly/ZLuC1*) for all Dart objects except null. The result is that a non-nullable object is a subclass of Object. As you become more familiar with writing Dart code, creating classes will become second nature. Object-oriented programming provides a means to model ideas and associate behavior. Classes provide a model in which you can define both the data and the functionality to access the incorporated data within the model.

In the Figure 5-2 example, the class is used to determine how many days are left in the week.

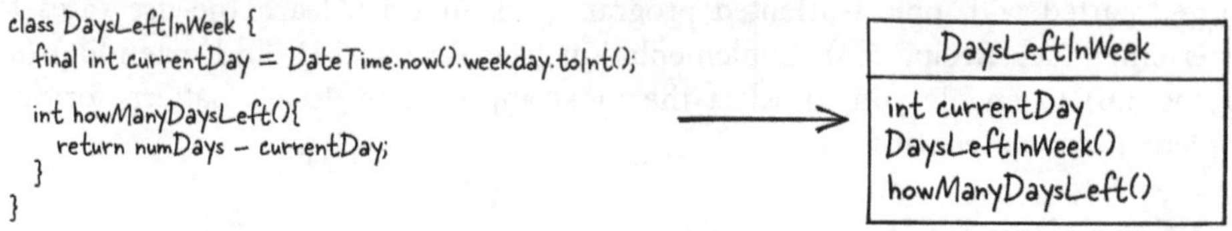

```
class DaysLeftInWeek {
  final int currentDay = DateTime.now().weekday.toInt();

  int howManyDaysLeft(){
    return numDays - currentDay;
  }
}
```

```
┌─────────────────────────┐
│     DaysLeftInWeek       │
├─────────────────────────┤
│ int currentDay          │
│ DaysLeftInWeek()         │
│ howManyDaysLeft()        │
└─────────────────────────┘
```

Figure 5-2. Class declaration

In the class definition shown in Figure 5-2, we see that we have the `currentDay` property and the `howManyDaysLeft` method.

The declaration uses "class" to denote the definition that follows, including elements for both variables and functions. A class constructor, `DaysLeftInWeek`, is given the same name as the class and is called when an object is instantiated. Use the class constructor to perform one-off activities when the class is to be created.

Within the class, the `currentDay` variable is declared as a final `int`, meaning its value will be determined at runtime and represent an integer. Additionally, there is a method declared `howManyDaysLeft` that is used to perform a calculation.

5.3 Initializing a Class Using a Constructor

Problem

You want to run a series of instructions each time a new object is created based on the class.

Solution

Use a class constructor to perform initialization of the object instance. The initialization can be used to set sensible defaults to class values.

Here's an example of how to declare and use a class constructor:[1]

```
const numDays = 7;

class DaysLeftInWeek {
  int currentDay = 0;

  DaysLeftInWeek(){
    currentDay = DateTime.now().weekday.toInt();
  }
```

---

1 In the example, the keyword `this` has been omitted from the `currentDay` variable assignment. Dart best practice indicates the keyword `this` should be omitted unless required.

```
    int howManyDaysLeft(){
      return numDays - currentDay;
    }
  }

  void main() {
    DaysLeftInWeek dayCalculator = DaysLeftInWeek();

    print ('Today is day ${dayCalculator.currentDay}');
    print ('${dayCalculator.howManyDaysLeft()} day(s) left in the week');
  }
```

Discussion

In the example, the class is used to determine how many days are left in the week. The declaration uses "class" to denote the definition that follows, including elements for both variables and functions.

In Figure 5-3, note that the class is declared by making a call to the class.

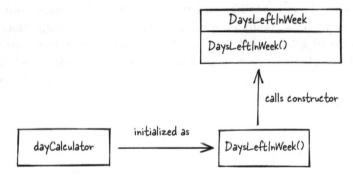

Figure 5-3. Class constructor initialization

A constructor takes the same name as the class and will be called upon instantiation of the class. In this instance, the constructor sets the class variable currentDay with the value of today's date. Within the class DaysLeftInWeek, note there is a function defined with the same name as the class.

To use the class, declare a variable (e.g., weekClass) to instantiate the DaysLeftIn Week class. From the declaration, the variable weekClass is able to access both the variable and functions associated with the class. Again, we use a final keyword to declare the weekClass and indicate the value is determined at runtime.

Finally, the print statements demonstrate how to access a variable and a function to access the underlying data. In both instances, the class value is derived from the variable weekClass. The currentDay and the method howManyDaysLeft are both able to retrieve the data associated with the class.

If you are familiar with other object-oriented languages, you may be surprised that the this keyword is omitted. Dart only requires the use of this to provide explicit guidance on the variable to be used (i.e., variable shadowing). Reference the Dart documentation (*https://dart.dev/guides*) on variable shadowing, which outlines how to avoid this situation.

5.4 Adding Class Inheritance

Problem

You want to enhance an existing class by introducing additional functionality that is not present in the original class.

Solution

Use a class with the extends keyword to incorporate inheritance from the parent class. When using the extends keyword, a subclass will inherit the superclass functionality. As an object-oriented language, Dart provides extensive class support in each new release. Here's an example of how to use extends to add class inheritance in Dart:

```
class Media {
  String title = "";
  String type = "";

  Media(){ type = "Class"; }

  void setMediaTitle(String mediaTitle){ title = mediaTitle; }

  String getMediaTitle(){ return title; }

  String getMediaType(){ return type; }
}

class Book extends Media {
  String author = "";
  String isbn = "";

  Book(){ type = "Subclass"; }

  void setBookAuthor(String bookAuthor){ author = bookAuthor; }

  void setBookISBN(String bookISBN){ isbn = bookISBN; }

  String getBookTitle(){ return title; }
```

```
    String getBookAuthor(){ return author; }

    String getBookISBN(){ return isbn; }
}

void main() {
  var myMedia = Media();

  myMedia.setMediaTitle('Tron');
  print ('Title: ${myMedia.getMediaTitle()}');
  print ('Type: ${myMedia.getMediaType()}');


  var myBook = Book();
  myBook.setMediaTitle("Jungle Book");
  myBook.setBookAuthor("R Kipling");
  print ('Title: ${myBook.getMediaTitle()}');
  print ('Author: ${myBook.getBookAuthor()}');
  print ('Type: ${myBook.getMediaType()}');
}
```

Discussion

In the code example, the Media class is extended through the Book subclass. As a parent class, the Media functionality will be available to any child class, as shown in Figure 5-4.

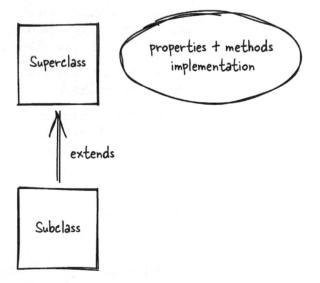

Figure 5-4. Class inheritance

Inheritance allows classes to assume the methods and properties of the superclass, as shown in Figure 5-4. The result is that the child and parent class support the same properties and methods.

Therefore, as illustrated in Figure 5-5, the Book class includes the properties and methods associated with Media in addition to whatever has been defined explicitly in the Book class.

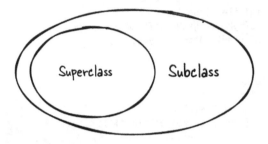

Figure 5-5. Class inheritance relationship

We create a child Book subclass that extends the Media class, meaning it can be used to access the methods and variables instantiated within it. When using a subclass, it is possible to override existing class functionality, e.g., methods, etc.

Extends provides general class inheritance where the parent (i.e., superclass) functionality is available to the child (i.e., subclass). The extends keyword relationship between parent and child is one to one, meaning multiple inheritance is not supported. When using this relationship, be aware that you will likely have a super.method() call to ensure the parent class is aware of changes made in the child.

Note: we do not redeclare setMediaTitle methods for Book. Instead, we can call this method from the Book class as if it had been explicitly declared.

Using extends is a useful approach where there are similar data structures available that potentially need slightly different methods. In the example, the Media class is a generic abstraction that is set up to hold base information. The Book class is a specialization of the Media class offering the ability to add book-specific information.

5.5 Adding a Class Interface

Problem

You want to use a class specification to outline the properties and methods to be declared when defining an object.

Solution

Use a class interface to define the specification for an object that must be adhered to by implementers. Here's an example of how to define an interface class in Dart:

```dart
abstract class Media {
  late String myId;
  late String myTitle;
  late String myType;

  void setMediaTitle(String mediaTitle);
  String getMediaTitle();

  void setMediaType(String mediaType);
  String getMediaType();

  void setMediaId(String mediaId);
  String getMediaId();
}

class Book implements Media {
  @override
  late String myId;
  @override
  late String myTitle;
  @override
  late String myType;

  @override
  void setMediaTitle(String mediaTitle) {
    myTitle = mediaTitle;
  }

  @override
  String getMediaTitle() {
    return myTitle;
  }

  @override
  void setMediaType(String mediaType) {
    myType = mediaType;
  }

  @override
  String getMediaType() {
    return myType;
  }

  @override
  void setMediaId(String mediaId) {
    myType = mediaId;
  }
```

```dart
  @override
  String getMediaId() {
    return myId;
  }

  Book(String mediaTitle, String mediaType, String mediaId) {
    myTitle = mediaTitle;
    myType = mediaType;
    myId = mediaId;
  }
}

void main() {
  final Book myBook =
      Book("Serverless Computing with Google Cloud", "Book", "ISBN-1111");

  print(myBook.getMediaTitle());
  print(myBook.getMediaType());
  print(myBook.getMediaId());
}
```

Discussion

In the code example, the Media class interface is used by the Book subclass. Media is a parent class, so its definitions will be available to any child class. Note the lack of implementation and initialization associated with the parent class. Instead, the implementation is left up to the user of the interface.

To use an interface class, use the implements keyword. If you are familiar with other languages, you may recognize the term *abstract class*. An abstract class provides the definition for a class but cannot be used to initiate an object.

In the example, an abstract class named Media creates a generic interface for media information, as shown as part of Figure 5-6. The Book class implements the Media class interface, meaning it is responsible for getting and setting the values named in the abstract class. Both properties and methods need to be defined where they override the values stated in the interface. Each value defined in the Book class that is defined in the Media class features the prefix @override, meaning the interface has already been defined.

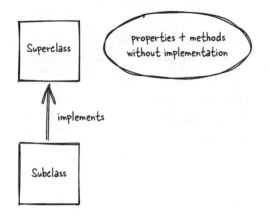

Figure 5-6. Class interface

Typically, an abstract interface will be used to define generic types that leave the implementation to the developer of the subclass to be defined. In Figure 5-7, the relationship between the superclass and subclass can be seen.

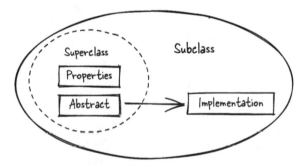

Figure 5-7. Class implements relationship

A subclass can implement multiple interfaces. However, when creating a subclass, you should be mindful not to make the class hierarchy overly complicated. Using a class interface requires you to implement the designated interface and comply with the signature used by the abstract class.

The typical use case for an interface definition is where implementation will be handled as a separate concern.

5.6 Adding a Class Mixin

Problem

You want an existing class to aggregate functionality from multiple class hierarchies.

Solution

Use *mixins* when requiring functionality from multiple classes. Mixins are a powerful tool when working with classes and allow information to be incorporated from multiple classes.

Here's an example of how to use a mixin:

```
abstract class SnickersOriginal {
  bool hasHazelnut = true;
  bool hasRice    = false;
  bool hasAlmond  = false;
}

abstract class SnickersCrisp {
  bool hasHazelnut = true;
  bool hasRice    = true;
  bool hasAlmond  = false;
}

class ChocolateBar {
  bool hasChocolate = true;
}

class CandyBar extends ChocolateBar with SnickersOriginal {
  List<String> ingredients = [];

  CandyBar(){
    if (hasChocolate){
      ingredients.add('Chocolate');
    }
    if (hasHazelnut){
      ingredients.add('Hazelnut');
    }
    if (hasRice){
      ingredients.add('Rice');
    }
    if (hasAlmond){
      ingredients.add('Almonds');
    }
  }

  List<String> getIngredients(){
    return ingredients;
  }
}

void main() {
  var snickersOriginal = CandyBar();
  print ('Ingredients:');
  snickersOriginal.getIngredients().forEach((ingredient) => print(ingredient));
}
```

Discussion

In the example, two abstract classes are defined to hold the information relating to variations on a Snickers chocolate bar. The main chocolate bar class does not contain the required functionality, so we incorporate a new class to extend the ability of the program. Figure 5-8 outlines how classes can be extended through the mixin keyword.

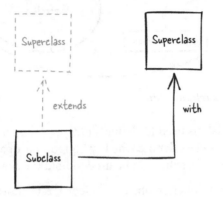

Figure 5-8. Class extends based on a mixin

The with keyword was only recently introduced to Dart; however, it is something developers have requested. If you work with the Flame game engine, you will use this keyword a lot. If you have worked in other languages, you may be more familiar with the term *mixin*, where multiple classes can be combined to provide additional functionality.

A mixin can be used with both inheritance and interface class definitions. To use the abstract class with the CandyBar class, we use a mixin. A mixin requires the use of the with keyword and combines class objects.

In Figure 5-9, the referenced superclasses should remain isolated, meaning classes used must not overlap. The base class of the CandyBar should not override the default constructor used in the abstract or parent class.

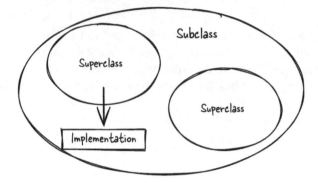

Figure 5-9. Class extends relationship

Typically, an abstract class is used to define a blueprint for an object to be created. In the example, the abstract class denotes the key ingredients of a candy bar. In addition, we create a chocolate bar class that can be used to hold the shared details.

Use a mixin to enable a subclass object to incorporate more functionality without having to write specific code. In the example, a combination of parent class with an abstract class allows distinct functionality to be merged. From this merge, the Candy Bar subclass is endowed with behavior relating to a chocolate bar and a variety of Snickers (i.e., Original over the Crisp version). Once the child subclass is created, it can be used to access the general ingredients of the candy bar.

## CHAPTER 6

Dart Test Cases

In this chapter, you will learn how to create test cases for your Dart-based code. Testing is a valuable stage of development that provides a link between application requirements and developed code. Testing is an important step in every developer's workflow. Ensuring that an application's behavior is aligned to a specification can significantly reduce the amount of effort to track defects. Defining guardrails for how an application should behave gives the developer confidence when making enhancements, as they are able to quickly identify whether a change breaks existing functionality.

Dart and Flutter share a test framework, so over the course of this chapter I begin the discussion on testing and its relevance to creating applications in Dart. Generally, Dart/Flutter testing can be broken down into three distinct types: unit, integration, and widget UI, as shown in Figure 6-1.

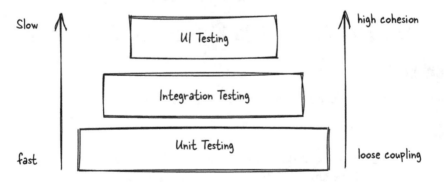

Figure 6-1. The test pyramid

In this chapter, we will cover the unit and integration aspects, which are the first two types of testing, as illustrated in Figure 6-1. The most common type of testing, from a developer perspective, is unit testing. A unit test compares an input to an individual function/class with the expected output. Such tests are run against the developed code and will typically report back as a pass/fail for the scenario presented.

The combination of unit and integration testing strategies provides a good foundation on which to validate that an application meets requirements. Over the course of this chapter we will use the following "travel.dart" sample application to demonstrate a few steps to create unit and integration tests. Create the dart file (*test_dart_sample/test_dart_sample.dart*) and add the following code:

```dart
const convertToKilometers = 1.60934;
const convertToMiles     = 0.62137119;

class Travel {
  late double distance;

  Travel(double newDistance) {
    distance = newDistance;
  }

  double distanceToMiles() {
    return distance * convertToMiles;
  }

  double distanceToKilometers() {
    return distance * convertToKilometers;
  }
}
```

In the sample code, the test performs a verification of distance conversion. The Travel class incorporates a constructor that will initialize the distance property based on the parameter used with the method. In addition, there are two methods used to convert the stored distance to kilometers and miles, respectively.

6.1 Adding the Dart Test Package to Your Application

Problem

You want a way to incorporate unit tests in your application.

Solution

Dart provides a test framework, meaning that test cases can easily be added to existing applications. We have already defined a template Flutter application earlier (see the chapter introduction). In order to use the Flutter test framework, add the *flutter_test/dart_test dev_dependencies* within the application *pubspec.yaml*. The packages provide the ability to incorporate testing as part of the development workflow.

Add the *test.dart* package to your application's *pubspec.yaml*. For further details on how to perform this task, see Recipe 8.5.

Here's an example of how to add the test package in Dart:

```
dart pub add test --dev
```

Discussion

Adding the Dart test package is performed in the same way as adding any other package. One thing to note is the use of the additional parameter --dev to indicate that the package is only required for the development phase.

Dart expects tests to be located in a test subfolder. From here, the unit tests can be split into multiple files or accessed as a single file. Review Recipe 6.3 to learn how to incorporate unit tests into your Dart application.

If you are using DartPad (*https://dartpad.dev*), you will need to use:

```
import 'package:flutter_test/flutter_test.dart';
```

The *flutter_test* package provides much the same functionality as *package:test/test.dart*, so you will still be able to test in this environment. However, you will need to have the test and application code located in a single file.

6.2 Creating a Sample Test Application

Problem

You want to develop a small class to use for working with the Dart testing package.

Solution

Create a Dart test file under the root folder of the application. In our example application, we have used the name *test_dart_sample.dart*. The resulting filename and path in your test environment will be *test_dart_sample/test_dart_sample.dart*.

Here's an example of our sample Dart code that will act as the basis of our tests:

```
const convertToKilometers = 1.60934;
const convertToMiles     = 0.62137119;

class Travel {
  late double distance;

  Travel(double newDistance) {
    distance = newDistance;
  }
```

```
  double distanceToMiles() {
    return distance * convertToMiles;
  }

  double distanceToKilometers() {
    return distance * convertToKilometers;
  }
}
```

Discussion

In the example code, a class is declared with a constructor and two methods that we will use to write tests throughout the chapter.

If you are working in an IDE such as Android Studio or VS Code, the code can be split across multiple files. Remember when using the DartPad (*https://dartpad.dev*) editor that it is limited to a single file, so you would need to place the base class and test code (featuring the main method) in the same file.

6.3 Running Unit Tests in Your Dart Application

Problem

You want a way to write unit tests for your Dart application.

Solution

Add a Dart unit test to your *test* directory. Tests can be defined to provide coverage of the element to be verified within your application.

A good approach when writing unit tests is to follow the arrange, act, and assert (AAA) pattern. The arrange phase sets up the values to be used and later validated. An act phase performs the action—in our example, a call to the `travel.distance` method. Finally, the assert phase completes the pattern by verifying that the result matches the expected outcome.

Our example uses the AAA pattern. The pattern prescribes each step of the test based on the preceding step to minimize errors. Following this approach makes our tests more straightforward to both read and maintain.

At this point, if you are using separate test and application code, your directory will be similar to the following outline:

```
.
├── analysis_options.yaml
├── bin
│   └── test_dart_sample.dart
```

```
├── CHANGELOG.md
├── lib
│   └── test_dart_sample.dart
├── pubspec.lock
├── pubspec.yaml
├── README.md
├── test
│   └── test_dart_sample_test.dart
└── test_dart_sample.iml
```

In the *test* directory, note that we will be using the application code defined in Recipe 6.1. If your code does not match that, replace/add the file named *test_dart_sample_test.dart* with the following content:

```dart
import 'package:test_dart_sample/test_dart_sample.dart';

void main() {
  test('Travel Distance', () {
    // Arrange
    var distance = 10.0;
    var expectedDistance = distance;

    // Act
    var travel = Travel(expectedDistance);
    var result = travel.distance;

    // Assert
    expect(expectedDistance, result);
  });
}
```

To run the test, use the `dart test` command to see the test completion results:

```
dart test
```

The result should indicate that all tests have successfully passed:

```
00:00 +0: Travel Distance
00:00 +1: All tests passed!
```

Discussion

In the example code we have one test defined; therefore, when we run the test, we should see a single test for the `Travel Distance` class. The result verifies that the `Travel` class object has been successfully initialized to the distance value.

In Figure 6-2, which shows the `Travel Distance` unit test, we perform a number of steps to verify that the `Travel` class performs as expected. First, we arrange the input to the condition we wish to test. Note that the distance is set to a variable. I do this so the rest of the test flows from a variable. If I then need to copy or change this unit test, I only need to amend a single distance variable rather than amend multiple values.

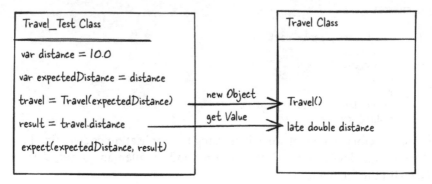

Figure 6-2. `Travel Distance` *unit test*

The act phase of the unit test performs our operation. Here we pass the distance to our `Travel` class and then record the distance in a result variable. I could just use the distance variable directly; however, using an intermediary result variable makes the code more readable and requires less maintenance, should I change the content.

Finally, we get to the assertion section. Based on the input, we anticipate that the `expectedDistance` and result will match. If they do, our test is marked as successful and we can move on. If the results do not match, we have caught an error early in development and can fix it there and then.

Generally we want our unit tests to be fast and independent from the environment they are running in. If you need to incorporate external factors (e.g., database connection, API calls), then these kinds of tests are better represented with integration tests; see Recipe 6.5.

Writing tests for Dart code will get you to think about the general structure of your code. I highly recommend adding unit tests to your code, as doing so will strengthen your understanding and increase your development skills.

6.4 Grouping Multiple Unit Tests

Problem

You want a way to perform multiple unit tests against your application code.

Solution

Creating multiple unit tests follows the same pattern as creating a single unit test (see Recipe 6.3). In the example, we use the AAA pattern, meaning we arrange a value, perform an action, and assert the validity of the outcome.

Here's an example of how to use multiple tests in Dart using our file named *travel_test.dart*:

```dart
import 'package:test_dart_sample/test_dart_sample.dart';
import 'package:test/test.dart';

void main() {
  test('Travel Distance', () {
    // Arrange
    var distance = 10.0;
    var expectedDistance = distance;

    // Act
    var travel = Travel(expectedDistance);
    var result = travel.distance;

    // Assert
    expect(expectedDistance, result);
  });

  test('Travel Distance to Miles', () {
    // Arrange
    var miles = 10.0;
    var expectedMiles = miles * convertToMiles;

    // Act
    var travel = Travel(miles);
    var result = travel.distanceToMiles();

    // Assert
    expect(expectedMiles, result);
  });

  test('Travel Distance to Kilometers', () {
    // Arrange
    var kilometers = 10.0;
    var expectedKiloMeters = kilometers * convertToKilometers;

    // Act
    var travel = Travel(kilometers);
    var result = travel.distanceToKilometers();

    // Assert
    expect(expectedKiloMeters, result);
  });
}
```

At this point, your directory will be similar to the following structure:

```
.
├── analysis_options.yaml
├── bin
│   └── test_dart_sample.dart
```

```
├── CHANGELOG.md
├── lib
│   └── test_dart_sample.dart
├── pubspec.lock
├── pubspec.yaml
├── README.md
├── test
│   └── test_dart_sample_test.dart
└── test_dart_sample.iml
```

To run the preceding test, use the `dart test` to run the code and see the results:

```
dart test
```

The result should indicate that all tests have successfully passed:

```
00:00 +0: Travel Distance
00:00 +1: All tests passed!
```

Discussion

In the example code we have three tests defined, as shown in Figure 6-3. Similar to the single run of a test, we initially verify that the `Travel` class object has been successfully initialized to the `distance` value. In addition, we also test the methods associated with conversion to miles and kilometers, respectively.

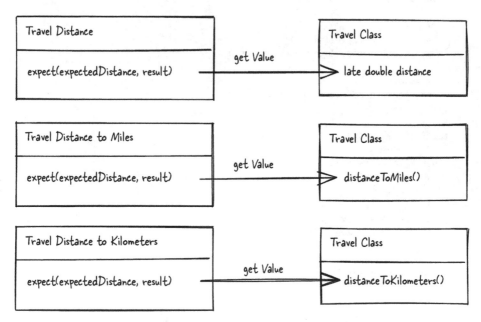

Figure 6-3. Multiple unit tests example

The additional tests for miles and kilometers both focus on their respective conversions. Figure 6-3 demonstrates how the AAA pattern provides a good foundation so that our tests follow a similar structure, despite verifying different outcomes.

Each test case is isolated, so if you need objects or variables to be initialized, that step needs to be performed as part of the test. It is a good approach to maintain simplicity in tests, as setting up complex scenarios can become hard to maintain over time.

When creating tests, you have the option of adding the test cases into a single file or breaking them out into multiple test files. Personally, I like to use a single file to directly link to a unit test file based on the convention of Dart file naming. So our *travel.dart* file would have a corresponding *travel_test.dart* file containing the relevant tests for that class definition.

6.5 Adding Mock Data for Testing

Problem

You do not have access to data required to test your application. Mock data can be incredibly useful where the underlying data is not available or is subject to a service constraint, such as when you are only allowed to call an API a certain number of times (i.e., API rate limiting).

Solution

Add a mock interface to your application to enable data requirements to be fulfilled with temporary data created specifically for testing.

Here's an example of how create a mock API call that returns some data:

```dart
import 'package:test_dart_sample/test_dart_sample.dart';
import 'package:test/test.dart';

Future <double> _loadResource(int testDelay) async {
  try {
    await Future.delayed(Duration(seconds: testDelay));
    return 10.0;
  } catch (e) {

    print(e);
    return 0.0;
  }
}

void main() {
  test('Travel Distance Delay', () async {
    // Arrange
    int customDelay = 5;
```

```
    var distance = await _loadResource(customDelay);
    var expectedDistance = distance;

    // Act
    var travel = Travel(expectedDistance);
    var result = travel.distance;

    // Assert
    expect(expectedDistance, result);
  });
}
```

To run the preceding test, use the `dart test` to run the code and see the results:

```
dart test
```

The result should indicate that all tests have successfully passed:

```
00:00 +0: Travel Distance Delay
00:05 +1: All tests passed!
```

Discussion

In the example code, a mock interface is added to replicate a situation where data is returned from an external query.

In Figure 6-4, the task is set to a customizable delay—in this instance, five seconds—to replicate a slow download experience. When the test is executed at the command line, you will see that the test experiences a delay of approximately five seconds to replicate a real-world download scenario. If you amend the delay, the time taken for the test will reflect the duration set for the delay value. You can learn more about how to incorporate a Future in Recipe 3.6.

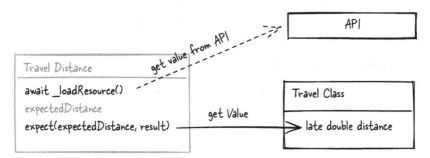

Figure 6-4. Using mock data for unit tests

To perform this activity to mock the retrieval of external data, use a Future to initiate an asynchronous task. An asynchronous operation is one where the program can complete other work while waiting for the completion of a task. Typically an asynchronous/async task will be accompanied by the `await` keyword, which indicates the return value may take some time to complete.

Introducing the mock response removes a blocker to development and also provides a simple mechanism to provide quality assurance. Adding a mock interface can provide an expedient method for working with external dependencies such as API or databases. Capturing the response from external dependencies allows you to create a mock interface that closely matches the type of response generated from the actual dependency.

A typical use case for this type of approach would be when you are working with resources that are not within your control as a developer (for example, if you are working with an API that is being developed but is not quite ready, or with a backend database).

## CHAPTER 7

Introducing the Flutter Framework

In this chapter, we begin our journey with the Flutter framework and focus on some of the fundamentals of Flutter.

For me, the best place to start a Flutter application is with a diagram of how your application will look and operate. If you come from a design background, you may be more familiar with the term *wireframe*. In either instance, we want to build a representative version of the application design.

Once you are more comfortable building out interfaces with Flutter, a good source of inspiration can be found on sites such as *dribbble.com*. I generally look at sites like this to figure out how a design could come together and then map out the requirement via a series of images (i.e., wireframes).

The Flutter team has your back, as they provide a wide range of templates to get you started coding your application. Once you have a starter code, it's time to understand the difference between stateful and stateless widgets, which will be a continual question as you build out your designs. Thankfully, Flutter's ability to create ever more complex interfaces means this investment in time really pays off.

When talking about Flutter, we really need to understand widgets and how they are used to render on-screen components. We start off by discussing mocking an interface and creating a boilerplate Flutter application before defining what a widget is; then we look at how widgets are used to make (compose) a user interface. Finally, we have a brief discussion of the widget tree structure to round off our understanding of the structure used within Flutter to represent the interaction between components.

7.1 Mocking an Application Interface

Problem

You want a way to mock an interface to understand layout before creating a Flutter application.

Solution

Use a graphics package to design your application. Building a wireframe of your application can help to solidify how the application works.

Here are some example packages that may be helpful, depending on your budget and use case:

Product	Link	Price	Description
Excalidraw	*https://excalidraw.com*	Free	A general web-based graphic design tool
Figma	*https://www.figma.com*	Free/Paid	A shared design and build solution for generating UI templates without code
FlutterFlow	*https://flutterflow.io*	Free/Paid	Interactive UI templates and components that generate Flutter code

Discussion

Mocking an interface is an excellent way to get started with a visual framework like Flutter. There are many ways to design an interface, ranging from free online tools to dedicated applications specifically created for Flutter.

When creating a mock of an application, I aim to capture the interface from the perspective of widgets to be used. Doing this makes it easier to build certain designs. If you are dealing with more complex designs, building an understanding of the application demands leads to a cleaner interface and design aesthetic.

Figure 7-1 is an example output using Excalidraw of the first Flutter application I created.

In the diagram, I include the functionality, i.e., two pages and a navigation bar. I also note how the screen transitions were meant to work. Breaking down the interface is a good way to learn how the various widgets interact. Also, learning the correct terminology for widgets, etc., helps to find the appropriate solution. While the application is not very sophisticated, it did help me to learn the fundamentals of widget construction using Flutter.

From the diagram you should be aware that this type of interface is very common among Flutter applications. Learning to incorporate widgets such as ListView, Text, and Image is essential, as is handling gestures and navigation.

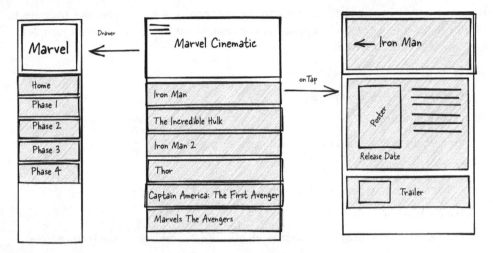

Figure 7-1. Wireframe mock-up design

7.2 Creating a Boilerplate Flutter Project

Problem

You want to create a new Flutter application based on a template.

Solution

Use a Flutter template to start your application. You don't have to start from scratch, because Flutter provides a range of application templates. There are a number of different templates available that provide a basic setup.

In more recent versions of the Flutter framework, work has been done to provide some feature-rich examples. Use this boilerplate code to improve your skills and understanding of common usage patterns from the experts.

Here are some templates available with the Flutter framework to get you started:

Type	Description
app	This is the default for `flutter create` and is used to generate a Flutter application.
module	This option will enable you to create a module that can be integrated with other applications.
package	This option will enable a shareable Flutter project.
plugin	This option provides an API base for use with Android and iOS.
skeleton	This option provides a best practice application based on a Detail View.

By appending the template command, i.e., `--template` or `-t`, you can indicate to Flutter that a template is to be applied at creation. What follows are some examples of how the templates are used.

To create the default application type:

```
flutter create my_awesome_app
```

To create a module:

```
flutter create -t module my_awesome_module
```

To create a package:

```
flutter create -t package my_awesome_package
```

To create a plug-in:

```
flutter create -t plugin my_awesome_plugin --platforms web --platform android
```

 When creating a plug-in, you must specify the platform to be supported. Each platform to be added requires the addition of the `--platform` prefix.

To create a skeleton:

```
flutter create -t skeleton my_awesome_skeleton
```

Discussion

In the examples shown, you will note that the Flutter tool provides a lot of boilerplate code to get you started. Central to this task is the command `flutter create`, which is meant to allow you to specify the type of code to be generated, e.g., module, package, plug-in.

`Flutter create` also has an option that can be applied to generate the code offline. To use this option, simply type **flutter create --offline [action]**. I find this option super handy when working in an environment that doesn't have a great internet connection. Your mileage may vary with this option, as it requires the pub cache to be available, and I have seen it occasionally fail when working in Android Studio.

When you create a project based on a template, you must consider the device currently available on your machine. In addition to templates, you may also reference sample code from the API documentation website (*http://docs.flutter.dev*). To use the code from the site, you need to reference the sample ID located on the page for the widget to be used. In the following example, the code can be found on the `Gesture Detector` class web page (*https://oreil.ly/_0SjI*):

```
flutter create -s widgets.GestureDetector.1 my_awesome_sample
```

Samples are available to provide a quick way to access the multitude of content available online. As a developer, I personally recommend targeting the web in addition to the desired host platform. Including the web makes sense, as it includes a very effective method of enabling application testing within a browser. Not to mention, it is super quick and easy to do incremental testing in a browser. During the development phase, this approach can certainly improve developer velocity for both small and large enhancements.

7.3 Removing the Flutter Debug Banner

Problem

You want a way to remove the debug banner from your Flutter application.

Solution

Use the `debugShowCheckModeBanner` to remove the debug banner applied to Flutter applications.

Here's an example Flutter application to demonstrate how to turn the `debug` property off:

```dart
import 'package:flutter/material.dart';

void main() {
  runApp(const MyApp());
}

class MyApp extends StatelessWidget {
  const MyApp({Key? key}) : super(key: key);

  @override
  Widget build(BuildContext context) {
    const title = 'Debug Example';

    return MaterialApp(
      title: title,
      home: Scaffold(
        appBar: AppBar(
          title: const Text(title),
        ),
        body: const Text("Removed Debug Banner"),
      ),
      debugShowMaterialGrid: false,
      debugShowCheckedModeBanner: false,
    );
```

```
      }
    }
```

Discussion

The example code demonstrates how to remove the debug flag from your application.

The debugShowCheckedModeBanner accepts a Boolean value to indicate whether the notification should be shown. In the example, the "Debug" message is turned off by setting the property to false.

Flutter has a default value of true set for the debugShowCheckedModeBanner. Developers are required to explicitly set this value as false to remove the temporary banner from applications. The following table outlines the various settings for the application states of Debug and Release:

Mode	Property	Discussion
Debug	debugShowCheckedModeBanner	The banner can be controlled via the Boolean value. Setting the property to true will show the banner; this is the default for new applications. Amending the property to false will remove the banner from your application.
Release	debugShowCheckedModeBanner	The banner is not displayed when in Release mode, irrespective of the property setting.

The debugShowMaterialGrid setting provides a grid overlay for your application. If you need to address a placement issue for the screen to be rendered, this setting is a useful option to temporarily enable in your application. The default property for this option is false, so you only need to enable it when required. To use this setting, your application needs to be in debug mode.

7.4 Recognizing Widgets

Problem

You want to understand how Flutter uses widgets to deliver a consistent view across multiple platforms.

Solution

Widgets are components that represent on-screen items such as Text, Images, and Lists. When starting with Flutter, it can be challenging to get your head around the fact that the majority of code represents a widget.

Discussion

The clever part of Flutter widgets is that they are composable, meaning you augment the functionality to create new widgets. Being able to build on existing widgets is incredibly powerful, as you don't have to resort to first principles and can get straight into using existing components.

The key thing to remember is that the widget class is an immutable description of the user interface that can be inflated into the elements associated with the render tree.

For the most part, when building a user interface you will be using/combining/creating new widgets to deliver the required functionality. The interesting aspect of this work is combining existing widgets to achieve a desired outcome.

7.5 Understanding the Widget Tree

Problem

You want to understand how Flutter uses a widget tree to compose the user interface.

Solution

Widgets are used by Flutter to compose a view within an application. Combining widgets is necessary to build rich user interfaces, and the connectivity between widgets is achieved with a tree structure. The view to be composed is dependent on the widgets used and the ordering applied.

Discussion

As denoted in the name, a widget tree builds relationships between the components used. A typical Flutter application will be based on a series of widgets, as shown in Figure 7-2.

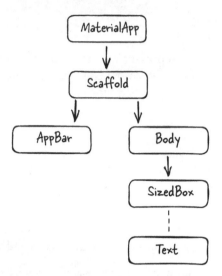

Figure 7-2. Widget tree

From the widget tree figure, we can see that the `MaterialApp` represents the parent for the application. From there, a `Scaffold` widget is used to branch to children that provide different functionality.

One of the most important aspects of developing with Flutter is refactoring your code to be sympathetic to the widget tree within your application. When starting out in Flutter, it is not uncommon to see very large widget trees similar to the one in Figure 7-2. A common approach is to separate out the build context (and more specifically the rendering loop) to enhance overall widget rendering performance. To get started on refactoring, see Recipe 9.4.

7.6 Improving Widget Render Performance

Problem

You want to understand how Flutter renders widgets to build more performant applications.

Solution

Flutter widgets are part of a rendering loop that is used to add the various components on-screen. As a widget can be parent to other widgets, it can sometimes be necessary to create a build context for performance needs. The build context effectively delegates the management of the associated widgets.

Discussion

If you create a very complex hierarchy, this can become an expensive relationship to maintain from the perspective of application performance. Whenever your application is called to render information, it will try to determine whether it has the most current information available or whether a refresh is necessary.

In Figure 7-3, the render loop will observe any state change associated with a widget. Where an update is found, this invokes a rebuild of the associated widget tree for the build context.

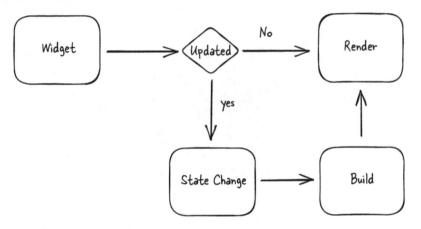

Figure 7-3. Flutter rendering loop

If your widget tree contains a large hierarchy, these will need to be rebuilt, which can impact overall application performance. Specifically, if you also incorporate state within your build context, this is one of the most common performance bottlenecks in Flutter development. Isolating state into a small build context will significantly improve overall performance, as the state change will be localized to only the relevant widget rather than an entire widget tree.

## CHAPTER 8

Adding Assets

In this chapter, we cover the addition of assets to your Flutter application. On many occasions you will want to host local application-based assets. Fortunately, Flutter incorporates a simple mechanism to achieve this through the *pubspec.yaml* file. You will learn how to:

- Create an assets folder
- Reference an image
- Reference an image folder
- Reference images in your application
- Add fonts to your application
- Import a package

Using assets is another step on the journey to understanding the Flutter environment. From personal experience, I always forget how to add images, so hopefully this will save you from my personal hell.

Adding assets provides a good way to reuse components, which easily extends the general functionality of your application. At the end of this chapter, you should have enough experience to effortlessly perform all of the tasks mentioned above in your future Flutter development journey.

8.1 Using the pubspec.yaml File

Problem

You want to understand what the *pubspec.yaml* file represents and how best to use it when developing in Flutter.

Solution

The *pubspec.yaml* file provides a centralized management file for the Flutter environment. In the file is a range of settings that include the SDK version being used, dependencies, assets location, and the name of the application.

Here's an example of a *pubspec.yaml* file:

```yaml
name: sample_app
description: A new Flutter project.

publish_to: 'none' # Remove this line if you wish to publish to pub.dev

version: 1.0.0+1

environment:
  sdk: '>=2.18.2 <3.0.0'

dependencies:
  flutter:
    sdk: flutter

  cupertino_icons: ^1.0.2

dev_dependencies:
  flutter_test:
    sdk: flutter

  flutter_lints: ^2.0.0

# The following section is specific to Flutter packages.
flutter:
  uses-material-design: true

  # To add assets to your application, add an assets section, like this:
  # assets:
  #   - images/a_dot_burr.jpeg
  #   - images/a_dot_ham.jpeg


  # fonts:
  #   - family: Schyler
  #     fonts:
  #       - asset: fonts/Schyler-Regular.ttf
  #       - asset: fonts/Schyler-Italic.ttf
  #         style: italic
  #   - family: Trajan Pro
  #     fonts:
  #       - asset: fonts/TrajanPro.ttf
  #       - asset: fonts/TrajanPro_Bold.ttf
  #         weight: 700
```

Discussion

In the example *pubspec.yaml* file, you will see the settings associated with a Flutter application. The file is a YAML file, meaning the formatting used is important, so take care when adding/amending entries.

The general format of the *pubspec.yaml* is as follows:

Field	Description
Name	Name of the application
Description	General overview of the application
Environment	SDK constraints
Dependencies	Package dependencies
Flutter	General assets for the application

If you do need to make a change in terms of packages, I personally recommend using the command line to run a `flutter pub add [package]` command, as this can be used to update the YAML file correctly. It can also be useful if you need to remove a package, i.e., `flutter pub remove [package]`.

When you need to update dependencies, use the `flutter pub get` command to reference the *pubspec.yaml* and update as required. Note: the above `flutter pub [option]` has an equivalent `dart pub [option]`.

8.2 Adding an Assets Folder

Problem

You want to add an assets folder to host information to be used in your Flutter application.

Solution

Adding a new folder to Flutter requires you to add a new directory to the existing folder containing your Flutter application. Flutter defaults to *[APP]/assets* for new content, so use that to minimize the work required to add new assets.

Here's an example of adding a new *images* folder:

1. Make a new subfolder under the root of the application. For example, for the application *sample_app*, it would be: *sample_app/assets*.
2. Within the assets folder, create a new subdirectory for images. The resulting folder structure should be: *sample_app/assets/images*.
3. Copy across the required images in the new *images* folder.

4. Update the *pubspec.yaml* to reference the *assets/images* directory created:

```
flutter:
  uses-material-design: true
  assets:
    - assets/images/
```

Discussion

In the preceding example, the environment has been updated to use an assets folder for images. When loading images, Flutter will try to be helpful in terms of assumptions for the location of the images to be used. Personally, I use the full path to avoid the dreaded "cannot find image" error message. Be aware that the access mechanism for the platform is different, so you may experience some inconsistencies.

Also note the subtle nuance between using a variable (part of your code) versus using the assets folder (part of your data). In the following example, rather than access an image, we use the assets folder to host a JSON file. The *pubspec.yaml* manifest would be updated as shown:

```
flutter:
  uses-material-design: true

  # To add assets to your application, add an assets section, like this:
  assets:
    - assets/example.json
```

The file is now accessible within your application and can be changed independently of the Flutter code used to access it. To access an asset declared in the *pubspec.yaml* file, use the `AssetBundle` object. See Recipe 13.4 for an example of how this can be used with a JSON file.

To see how to reference an asset image within a Flutter application, see Recipe 8.3.

8.3 Referencing an Image

Problem

You have created an assets folder loaded with images and want to reference an image in your application.

Solution

Adding an asset image to your application requires the path of the image to be displayed. To get the necessary image, consider using the *image* path to ensure the location is correctly used.

In our example *assets/images* folder, we have placed an image file named *green-tile.png*. Here's an example of how to display that image file using the Flutter framework:

```
import 'package:flutter/material.dart';

void main() {
  runApp(const MyApp());
}

class MyApp extends StatelessWidget {
  const MyApp({Key? key}) : super(key: key);

  @override
  Widget build(BuildContext context) {
    const title = 'Image Asset demo';

    return MaterialApp(
      title: title,
      home: Scaffold(
        appBar: AppBar(
          title: const Text(title),
        ),
        body: const MyImageAssetWidget(),
      ),
    );
  }
}

class MyImageAssetWidget extends StatelessWidget {
  const MyImageAssetWidget({Key? key}) : super(key: key);

  @override
  Widget build(BuildContext context) {
    return const Center(
      child: Image.asset('images/green-tile.png'),
    );
  }
}
```

Discussion

In the example, the code demonstrates how to reference an image located in the application assets folder. The image is referenced as being in the *images* subfolder, so it is prefixed with the label *images*.

When adding images to your application, ensure you restart your application (i.e., stop, then start) before attempting to access the asset items. A running application includes the application state minus the new assets; therefore, it will not be able to access items not previously available. To correctly reference the new assets being added, you are required to fully restart the application.

Flutter assumes assets such as images/fonts are located in the assets folder. If you intend to use an alternative location for your images outside of the assets folder, you will need to use the full path associated with the file.

8.4 Incorporating the Google Fonts Package

Problem

You want to add a package to use external fonts in a Flutter application.

Solution

Flutter allows you to incorporate external fonts as part of your application. Here's how to add the Google Fonts (*https://fonts.google.com*) package to the Flutter *pubspect.yaml* file:

```
  .
  .
  .
dependencies:
  flutter:
    sdk: flutter

  cupertino_icons: ^1.0.2
  google_fonts: 2.2.0
```

Discussion

To find information on available packages, a good place to start is the *pub.dev* site. The *pub.dev* site is a general website specifically for accessing assets to be used with Flutter and Dart. You can learn how to use a specific package by viewing the instructions on the site, which typically provides information such as installation instructions, a developer overview, and the platforms supported (e.g., iOS, Android, web). There are some general assumptions regarding placement and updates made, so it is worthwhile becoming familiar with how to integrate an external package with your application.

One of the places folks become confused is the addition to the pubspec dependencies section. The section to be updated is based on what entry you intend to make. For the addition of fonts, the addition already has an entry for Cupertino Fonts, so in this instance you can just add the Google Fonts entry below this setting.

8.5 Importing a Package

Problem

You want to incorporate functionality derived from a library.

Solution

Use a package to incorporate preexisting functionality into a Dart application.

`Import` statements enable external packages to be used within a Dart application. To utilize a package within an application, use the `import` statement to include the library.

Dart has a feature-rich set of libraries, which are packages of code for a particular task. These libraries are published on sites such as *pub.dev*. Use the package repository to find and import packages for a specific task to reduce development time.

Here's an example of how to use an `import` in Dart:

```
import 'dart:math';

void main() {

  // Generate random number between 0-9
  int seed = Random().nextInt(10);

  print ('Seed: $seed');
}
```

Discussion

In the preceding example code, we are importing the *dart:math* library. Dart uses the pub package manager to handle dependencies. The command line supports downloading of the appropriate package. Some IDEs also provide the ability to load information. In the example shown, *dart:math* is bundled with the SDK, so it does not need additional dependencies to be added.

Where an external package is used, a *pubspec.yaml* file will need to be defined to indicate information about that package. A *pubspec.yaml* file is metadata about the library being used. The file uses YAML format and enables dependencies to be listed in a consistent manner. For example, the *google_fonts* package would use the following declaration in the *pubspec.yaml* definition:

```
dependencies:
  google_fonts: ^2.1.0
```

In the Dart source code, the import statement can then reference the package:

```
import 'package:google_fonts/google_fonts.dart';
```

Pubspec.yaml is a position-based script, so code needs to be placed in a specific column for it to work. Most Flutter/Dart environments will tell you if you get this wrong, but it is easy to make a mistake. A more foolproof method is to use the command line to import new packages, as these will automatically be correctly aligned.

CHAPTER 9

Working with Widgets

In this chapter, we continue our journey with the Flutter framework. We now progress to a high-level overview of the most common widgets.

Widgets are an essential concept in Flutter and provide the basis of most applications. Learning how to integrate the numerous widget types available will significantly enhance your development skills. You will learn:

- What a Scaffold widget is
- How to refactor widgets for better build context performance
- What stateless and stateful widgets are
- How to build interfaces using Row and Column widgets

Refactoring your code is a skill that I highly recommend to avoid bugs and aid general performance. The chapter takes a brief moment to look at refactoring widgets. A widget represents a customizable user interface element, and Flutter provides the flexibility to build out beautiful interfaces without too much effort.

A strong point of Flutter is its ability to enable you to build feature-rich and beautiful interfaces very quickly. Making steady improvements in your code will also build your confidence and provide the least resistance path to working on more complex applications. Over the course of this chapter, we will continue our journey to explore the variety of widgets available to Flutter.

9.1 Creating a Stateless Widget in Flutter

Problem

You do not need to save state (i.e., save a value) associated with on-screen content.

Solution

Use a stateless widget to render on-screen content.

Here's an example of how to use a stateless widget in Flutter:

```
import 'package:flutter/material.dart';

void main() {
  runApp(const MyApp());
}

class MyApp extends StatelessWidget {
  const MyApp({Key? key}) : super(key: key);

  @override
  Widget build(BuildContext context) {
    const title = 'Stateless Widget demo';

    return MaterialApp(
      title: title,
      home: Scaffold(
        appBar: AppBar(
          title: const Text(title),
        ),
        body: const MyTextWidget(),
      ),
    );
  }
}

class MyTextWidget extends StatelessWidget {
  const MyTextWidget({Key? key}) : super(key: key);

  @override
  Widget build(BuildContext context) {
    return const Center(
      child: Text('Hello'),
    );
  }
}
```

Discussion

In the example, the StatelessWidget class is used to render a Text widget. A stateless widget essentially means that the retention of a value is not required. Typically, we use state to mean a value that needs to be maintained, such as an on-screen counter.

In the example, there is no state to store, as illustrated in Figure 9-1. Working without state makes your application architecture significantly simpler, as you have a lot less to consider. If you can, try to implement as much of your application as possible as a stateless design to reduce the overall complexity when developing code.

Figure 9-1. Stateless widget example

There may be times where it is necessary to save state; in this situation, see Recipe 9.2. Flutter is super flexible in regard to the interaction between stateless and stateful, so don't be under the impression that you need to select one or the other.

9.2 Creating a Stateful Widget in Flutter

Problem

You want to store a state (i.e., a value) that is associated with a Flutter widget.

Solution

Use the Flutter `StatefulWidget` to store and retain a value within an application. The declaration of a stateful widget indicates that a value is to be retained.

Here's an example of using a stateful widget to hold the state:

```
import 'package:flutter/material.dart';

void main() {
  runApp(const MyApp());
}

class MyApp extends StatelessWidget {
  const MyApp({Key? key}) : super(key: key);
```

```
      @override
      Widget build(BuildContext context) {
        const title = 'Stateless Widget demo';

        return MaterialApp(
          title: title,
          home: Scaffold(
            appBar: AppBar(
              title: const Text(title),
            ),
            body: const MyTextWidget(),
          ),
        );
      }
    }

    class MyTextWidget extends StatefulWidget {
      const MyTextWidget({Key? key}) : super(key: key);

      @override
      _MyTextWidget createState() => _MyTextWidget();
    }

    class _MyTextWidget extends State<MyTextWidget> {
      int count = 0;

      @override
      Widget build(BuildContext context){
        return GestureDetector(
          onTap: () {
            setState((){
              count++;
            });
          },
          child: Center(child: Text('Click Me: $count')),
        );
      }
    }
```

Discussion

In the example, a stateful widget is created to retain the value associated with the user clicking on-screen text. The value associated with the text will increment on each click.

In Figure 9-2, an application event is triggered each time the user taps on the Text Widget. The event registers a tap and performs a setState call incrementing the count value by one. Amending the state automatically initiates a refresh of the build context, meaning the on-screen view will be refreshed and show the new value for count.

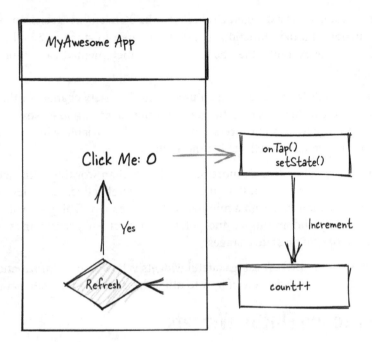

Figure 9-2. Stateful widget example

State management in Flutter typically utilizes the pattern shown in Figure 9-3. A stateful widget requires the creation of a few methods that are used to retain information.

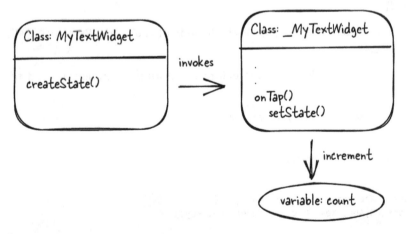

Figure 9-3. Stateful widget interaction

The class `MyTextWidget` stateful widget implements a `createState` method. The value returned from this method is assigned to a private variable, i.e., `_MyTextWidget`. In Flutter, private variables are prefixed with the underscore character. Observe how the private variable is constructed similarly to the stateless widgets seen previously. The introduction of a new function, `setState`, is used to store a value based on an `onTap` event. In the example, the `count` variable is incremented each time an `onTap` event is triggered.

The private class `_MyTextWidget` is then used to initiate state change. In the diagram, we can see that the `onTap()` is used to increment the `count` variable. Now when a user of the application interacts and presses the button, the variable will be incremented and the state change will be reflected in the application.

Working with stateful widgets is more of a challenge than working with stateless, but with some consideration of design, it can be just as effective. As a developer, you should be in a position to design a minimal state application. Doing so will reduce the overall complexity and minimize the potential impact on performance associated with redraw to update on state changes.

Another consideration when using stateful widgets is how to pass information. Reference Recipe 12.6 for an overview of how to utilize keys to communicate parameters.

9.3 Refactoring Flutter Widgets

Problem

You want a way to improve the readability of code.

Solution

Use refactoring to improve the general reliability of your code. Refactoring allows you to simplify code.

Here's an example of Flutter code before refactoring is applied around the `Build` function:

```
import 'package:flutter/material.dart';

void main() {
  runApp(const MyApp());
}

class MyApp extends StatelessWidget {
  const MyApp({Key? key}) : super(key: key);

  @override
  Widget build(BuildContext context) {
    const title = 'Image Widget';

    return MaterialApp(
      title: title,
```

```
        home: Scaffold(
          appBar: AppBar(
            title: const Text(title),
          ),
          body: Container(
            width: 200,
            height: 180,
            color: Colors.black,
            child: Column(
              children: [
                Image.network('https://oreil.ly/O4PEn'),
                const Text(
                  'itemTitle',
                  style: TextStyle(fontSize: 20, color: Colors.white),
                ),
                const Text(
                  'itemSubTitle',
                  style: TextStyle(fontSize: 16, color: Colors.grey),
                ),
              ],
            ),
          ),
        ),
      );
    }
}
```

Here's an example showing the same code, this time featuring refactoring used to create a new build context:

```
import 'package:flutter/material.dart';

void main() {
  runApp(const MyApp());
}

class MyApp extends StatelessWidget {
  const MyApp({Key? key}) : super(key: key);

  @override
  Widget build(BuildContext context) {
    const title = 'Image Widget';

    return MaterialApp(
      title: title,
      home: Scaffold(
        appBar: AppBar(
          title: const Text(title),
        ),
        body: MyContainerWidget(),
      ),
    );
  }
```

```
  }

class DataItem {
  final String title;
  final String subtitle;
  final String url;

  const DataItem({
    required this.title,
    required this.subtitle,
    required this.url,
  });
}

class DataView {
  final DataItem item = const DataItem(
      title: 'Hello',
      subtitle: 'subtitle',
      url: 'https://oreil.ly/O4PEn');
}

class MyContainerWidget extends StatelessWidget {
  MyContainerWidget({Key? key}) : super(key: key);

  final DataView data = DataView();

  @override
  Widget build(BuildContext context) {
    return Container(
      width: 200,
      height: 180,
      color: Colors.black,
      child: Column(
        children: [
          Image.network(data.item.url),
          Text(
            data.item.title,
            style: const TextStyle(fontSize: 20, color: Colors.white),
          ),
          Text(
            data.item.subtitle,
            style: const TextStyle(fontSize: 16, color: Colors.grey),
          ),
        ],
      ),
    );
  }
}
```

Discussion

In the example, two pieces of code are displayed to illustrate how refactoring can be used in your code. Readability is a broad subject and beyond the scope of this book. Put simply, we are referring to whether the meaning of the code can be easily discerned.

There are a couple of things to note in the original code that require refactoring. The associated widget tree has a single build context, so we should look to fix that. Data used in the application is embedded within the application code, which will make it difficult to update and maintain.

Our first step in refactoring is to introduce a new stateless widget. The widget will be responsible for the Scaffold body section. Adding a new stateless widget provides separation of code and also provides a new isolated build context. Our original widget tree now has a build context for the Scaffold and the new widget. Making this separation of build context will improve Flutter rendering performance (see Recipe 9.3).

The second change relates to management of the data. Embedding data within code is something that should be avoided, as it leads to maintenance issues and difficulty reading the code. Instead, consider creating separation for the data required. In the example, we create two new classes to host the data. `DataItem` is a general data class used to specify the data structure holding our application data. `DataView` is used to define the implementation, that is, how the data will be used within the application. In our example, we use `DataView` to declare a single item.

Overall, the changes made ensure that when you are creating and using the `MyContainerWidget` the process is both consistent and repeatable. As a developer making reference to `MyContainerWidget`, you now only need to be aware of the data requirement and the class invocation. Ultimately, based on the changes made, you now have two classes representing the data and implementation.

9.4 Using the Scaffold Class

Problem

You want to take advantage of the Flutter framework to define a consistent code structure for your application.

Solution

Use the Scaffold class to provide the high-level structure for your application. Scaffold implements the basic Material Design visual layout structure. By integrating the Scaffold widget, you have access to a rich API ready-made to show drawers, app bars, snack bars, and bottom navigation.

Here's an example of a Scaffold widget that is used to render a simple interface to the user:

```dart
import 'package:flutter/material.dart';

void main() => runApp(const MyApp());

class MyApp extends StatelessWidget {
  const MyApp({Key? key}) : super(key: key);

  static const String _title = 'Example';

  @override
  Widget build(BuildContext context) {
    return const MaterialApp(
      title: _title,
      home: MyStatelessWidget(),
    );
  }
}

class MyStatelessWidget extends StatelessWidget {
  const MyStatelessWidget({Key? key}) : super(key: key);

  @override
  Widget build(BuildContext context) {
    return Scaffold(
      appBar: AppBar(title: const Text('Scaffold Example')),
      backgroundColor: Colors.blueGrey,
      bottomNavigationBar: const BottomAppBar(
        color: Colors.blueAccent,
        shape: CircularNotchedRectangle(),
        child: SizedBox(
          height: 300,
          child: Center(child: Text("bottomNavigationBar")),
        ),
      ),
      body: _buildCardWidget(),
    );
  }

  Widget _buildCardWidget() {
    return const SizedBox(
      height: 200,
      child: Card(
        child: Center(
          child: Text('Top Level Card'),
        ),
      ),
    );
  }
}
```

Discussion

In the example, the Scaffold widget defines the screen layout for the developer to utilize common layout patterns. The elements are built into the Scaffold widget, so they can be used or not as you see fit.

In Figure 9-4, the main elements of a Scaffold widget are displayed. If you implement AppBar, Body, and Bottom Navigation elements, these will be rendered correctly on-screen without additional effort. Scaffold will expand to use the available on-screen space, meaning it will fill the entire screen.

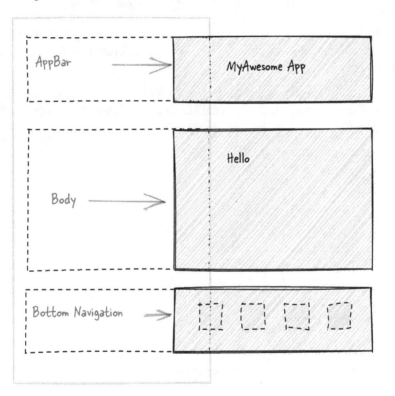

Figure 9-4. A Scaffold widget

Application behavior to set up important components is desirable, as you will use the Flutter framework to perform some intelligent management of on-screen arrangement. If an on-screen keyboard is present, the default Scaffold will adjust dynamically without additional logic being added to your application.

In general, avoid nesting the Scaffold class, as it is designed to be a top-level container for a MaterialApp. Scaffold provides the ability to enhance your application with AppBar (see Recipe 9.5) and Drawer widgets (Recipe 12.3). If you wish to use Scaffold with a FloatingActionButton, ensure you use a stateful widget (Recipe 7.4) to retain the associated button state.

9.5 Adding an AppBar Header

Problem

You want to incorporate an AppBar header section at the top of your application.

Solution

Use an AppBar widget to control the header section of your application. The AppBar is a versatile widget that enables developers to include links and additional functionality on-screen.

Here's an example of an AppBar widget that has a custom color applied to it. In addition, the header incorporates the optional elements of a leading icon (on the left-hand side) and an actions icon (on the right-hand side):

```
import 'package:flutter/material.dart';

void main() {
  runApp(const MyApp());
}

class MyApp extends StatelessWidget {
  final String titleAppBar = 'AppBar Demo';
  const MyApp({Key? key}) : super(key: key);

  @override
  Widget build(BuildContext context) {
    return MaterialApp(
      debugShowCheckedModeBanner: false,
      title: titleAppBar,
      home: Scaffold(
        appBar: MyAppBar(title:titleAppBar),
      ),
    );
  }
}


class MyAppBar extends StatelessWidget implements PreferredSizeWidget {

  final String title;
  final double sizeAppBar = 200.0;

  const MyAppBar({Key? key, required this.title}) : super(key: key);

  @override
```

```
    Size get preferredSize => Size.fromHeight(sizeAppBar);

    @override build(BuildContext context) {

      return AppBar(
        title: Text(title),
        backgroundColor: Colors.black,
        elevation: 10.0,
        leading: IconButton(onPressed: (){}, icon: const Icon(Icons.menu)),
        actions: [IconButton(onPressed: (){},
          icon: const Icon(Icons.settings))
        ],
      );
    }
  }
```

Discussion

In the preceding example, the AppBar (*https://oreil.ly/o3x_l*) widget has been moved
to its own class. I took this optional step to simplify the code and also demonstrate
how this action is performed.

In Figure 9-5, the elements of an AppBar widget are denoted by arrows. The AppBar
leading property provides the menu item on the left. The title is placed in the center,
with the actions menu option placed on the right.

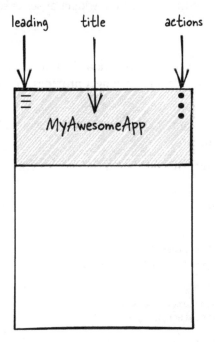

Figure 9-5. AppBar widget example

To include a menu option, you can use the `leading` property to add icons to the left-hand side of the interface. You are able to override the default behavior of Flutter and replace icons as desired. Actions buttons are typically associated with application configuration. Add these to the interface to provide further interaction, such as a settings option.

Using an AppBar provides access to a number of additional properties and methods. Typically, developers will use the main properties such as `Title`, `backgroundColor`, and `elevation`. In addition, you can also set the `backgroundColor` property of the AppBar directly to use a range of available colors. In the example, the `color` has been updated to `black`. An `elevation` property can also be used to display a flat (zero) or raised (>zero) graphical interface for that subtle graphical impact.

The AppBar requires an awareness of the dimensions for the header to be used. To address this, we call a static AppBar and use this to provide the appropriate dimension for our widget. The `preferredSize` is dynamic and will resize based on the content to be displayed.

9.6 Building with a Container

Problem

You want a way to isolate settings for a child widget or series of widgets.

Solution

Use a Container widget to provide a constrained space (e.g., padding, border, colors) for other child widgets. The Container widget provides a defined structure in which to place other widgets.

Here's an example using a Container widget to define an area that in turn has another smaller container defined:

```
import 'package:flutter/material.dart';

void main() {
  runApp(const MyApp());
}

class MyApp extends StatelessWidget {
  const MyApp({Key? key}) : super(key: key);

  @override
  Widget build(BuildContext context) {
    const title = 'Container Widget Demo';

    return MaterialApp(
```

```
        title: title,
        home: Scaffold(
          appBar: AppBar(
            title: const Text(title),
          ),
          body: const MyContainerWidget(),
        ),
      );
    }
  }

  class MyContainerWidget extends StatelessWidget {
    const MyContainerWidget({Key? key}) : super(key: key);

    @override
    Widget build(BuildContext context) {
      return Container(
        alignment: Alignment.center,
        height: 200,
        width: 200,
        color: Colors.red[300],
        child: Container(
          height: 100,
          width: 100,
          color: Colors.yellow,
        ),
      );
    }
  }
```

Discussion

In the example code, the Container widget is used to create a graphic based on a set dimension.

Figure 9-6 shows that the Container presents a constraint based on the `height` and `width` properties. Any child of the Container should also be constrained by these properties, meaning the Container parent size can be used to ratio widget space on-screen.

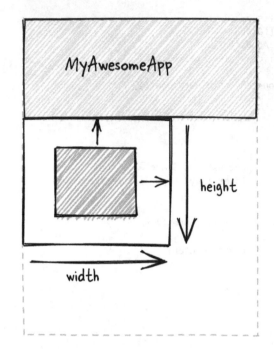

Figure 9-6. Container widget example

The parent container is given an alignment of center to ensure its children start at the middle of the container dimensions. Both height and width are defined for the parent to produce a square, with a color of red applied.

A second container is defined as a child, with a smaller dimension applied. The parent container has size constraints, so the second container should be set to recognize this and set its size accordingly. The second container can choose to ignore the sizing constraint and set a larger number than the parent, in which case the parent would be obscured by the child. As before, the container is given a color, this time yellow. The color applied is arbitrary and is used to differentiate the child from the parent.

When you specify the size and height of the parent widget, note that the child will be constrained to the dimensions set. In the example, the child container is given width and height attributes that are smaller than those of the parent. If the child container was not given these attributes, it would assume the parent dimensions and you would only see the yellow container when the application is run.

At this point you are probably thinking, well, what happens if I don't specify the height and width dimensions for the parent widget? The Container widget is aware of its environment and will take its parent dimensions from the existing viewport, that is, the application body. So in this scenario, you would see a red container taking up the majority of the screen.

Containers are super useful; however, they are not useful in every situation. If you want to provide whitespace in an application, the recommended approach is to use SizedBox (Recipe 9.8) rather than a Container widget.

9.7 Using a Center Widget

Problem

You want to ensure that information is centered on-screen.

Solution

Use the Center widget to align a child element on-screen.

Here's an example of how to use the Center widget to align on the intersection between the horizontal and vertical axes:

```
import 'package:flutter/material.dart';

void main() => runApp(const MyApp());

class MyApp extends StatelessWidget {
  const MyApp({Key? key}) : super(key: key);

  static const String _title = 'Center Widget Demo';

  @override
  Widget build(BuildContext context) {
    return const MaterialApp(
      title: _title,
      home: MyStatelessWidget(),
    );
  }
}

class MyStatelessWidget extends StatelessWidget {
  const MyStatelessWidget({Key? key}) : super(key: key);

  @override
  Widget build(BuildContext context) {
    return Scaffold(
      appBar: AppBar(title: const Text('Center Example')),
      body: _buildCenterWidget(),
    );
  }

  Widget _buildCenterWidget() {
    return const Center(
      child: Text(
        "Top Five Spoken Languages - 2022",
```

```
        style: TextStyle(fontSize: 30, color: Colors.grey),
      ),
    );
  }
}
```

Discussion

In the example, the code demonstrates the application of the Center widget to a Text widget on-screen. The Center widget ensures the text moves directly to the center of the available screen space indicated by the Scaffold body element, as shown in Figure 9-7.

Figure 9-7. Center text example output

The example illustrates how the Center widget can be used to align on-screen content. In most situations you will need to combine this widget with other techniques to achieve the desired outcome.

The Center widget provides a great way to center on-screen objects. While it is relatively straightforward to use in an application, do not underestimate the power it provides. It can be used in conjunction with a wide range of widgets to deliver different results. In more complex layouts, it may not be the single solution required, but it will most definitely save you time during your development phase.

9.8 Using a SizedBox

Problem

You want to add whitespace to a user interface.

Solution

Use the SizedBox widget to apply a defined space to the on-screen interface.

Here's an example in which we apply a defined layout to the user interface. A Sized-Box is used to structure the layout, complete with `width` and `height` settings:

```
import 'package:flutter/material.dart';

void main() => runApp(const MyApp());

class MyApp extends StatelessWidget {
  const MyApp({Key? key}) : super(key: key);

  static const String _title = 'SizedBox Widget Demo';

  @override
  Widget build(BuildContext context) {
    return const MaterialApp(
      title: _title,
      home: MyStatelessWidget(),
    );
  }
}

class MyStatelessWidget extends StatelessWidget {
  const MyStatelessWidget({Key? key}) : super(key: key);

  @override
  Widget build(BuildContext context) {
    return Scaffold(
      appBar: AppBar(title: const Text('SizedBox Example')),
      body: _buildSizedBoxWidget(),
    );
  }

  Widget _buildSizedBoxWidget() {
    return SingleChildScrollView(
      padding: const EdgeInsets.all(10.0),
      child: Column(
        children: const [
          SizedBox(
            width: 200,
            height: 100,
            child: Card(
```

```
            color: Colors.amber,
            child: Center(child: Text('Developer'))),
      ),
      SizedBox(
        width: 300,
        height: 100,
        child: Card(
            color: Colors.green,
            child: Center(child: Text('Flutter Framework'))),
      ),
      SizedBox(
        width: 400,
        height: 100,
        child: Card(
            color: Colors.blue,
            child: Center(child: Text('Dart SDK'))),
      ),
    ],
  ),
);
}
}
```

Discussion

In the example, a SizedBox is used in a couple of ways due to its versatility. In Figure 9-8, three SizedBox widgets are used to illustrate the interaction between developer, Flutter, and Dart.

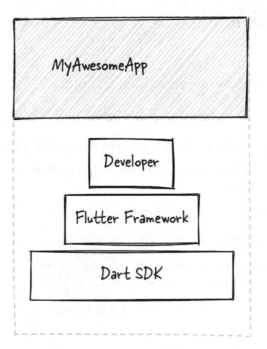

Figure 9-8. SizedBox example widget

A common use of SizedBox is to provide a fine control over layout between widgets. As SizedBox supports both `height` and `width` properties, you can achieve very fine control over positional elements on-screen.

However, SizedBox can be used in a wide variety of situations that you might see a Container widget used in. If your application just requires whitespace (i.e., a gap filler of a certain proportion), the recommendation is to use SizedBox. This recommendation is based on a performance comparison between the two widgets, where SizedBox has a (slight) advantage.

Think of SizedBox as an improved Container widget and you will most likely be on the correct track. Therefore, avoid combining SizedBox and Container widgets—use one or the other. In addition to `height` and `width`, SizedBox also supports the `child` property to enable expansion to include other widgets.

As a whitespace widget, SizedBox is purposely not visible by default. However, it does support a `child` element to allow you to embed other widgets within it. In the example code, the SizedBox incorporates a Card widget using the `child` property, so a color can be applied. If you need a color to be applied, you might still consider using a Container, as this is not supported by default within a SizedBox. To learn more about the Container widget, see Recipe 9.6.

9.9 Using a Column

Problem

You need a flexible widget to present as a vertical layout on-screen.

Solution

Use a Column widget to allow information to be displayed as a vertical array.

Here's an example of how to use the Column widget in Flutter to render content in a responsive manner on-screen:

```dart
import 'package:flutter/material.dart';

void main() => runApp(const MyApp());

class MyApp extends StatelessWidget {
  const MyApp({Key? key}) : super(key: key);

  static const String _title = 'Center Widget Demo';

  @override
  Widget build(BuildContext context) {
    return const MaterialApp(
      title: _title,
      home: MyStatelessWidget(),
    );
  }
}

class MyStatelessWidget extends StatelessWidget {
  const MyStatelessWidget({Key? key}) : super(key: key);

  @override
  Widget build(BuildContext context) {
    return Scaffold(
      appBar: AppBar(title: const Text('Center Example')),
      body: _buildCenterWidget(),
    );
  }

  Widget _buildCenterWidget() {
    return Column(
      children: [
        const SizedBox(height: 10.0),
        const Center(
            child: Text("Top Five Spoken Languages - 2022",
                style: TextStyle(fontSize: 30, color: Colors.grey))),
        const SizedBox(height: 20.0),
        SingleChildScrollView(
```

```
scrollDirection: Axis.horizontal,
child:
    Column(crossAxisAlignment: CrossAxisAlignment.start, children: [
  Row(children: [
    const SizedBox(
      width: 100.0,
      child: Text("English"),
    ),
    Container(
      width: 600.0,
      color: Colors.green,
      child: const Center(
          child: Text("1.3 Billion",
              style: TextStyle(fontSize: 18, color: Colors.white))),
    ),
  ]),
  const SizedBox(height: 10.0),
  Row(children: [
    const SizedBox(
      width: 100.0,
      child: Text("Mandarin"),
    ),
    Container(
      width: 550.0,
      color: Colors.orange,
      child: const Center(
          child: Text("1 Billion",
              style: TextStyle(fontSize: 18, color: Colors.white))),
    ),
  ]),
  const SizedBox(height: 10.0),
  Row(children: [
    const SizedBox(
      width: 100.0,
      child: Text("Hindi"),
    ),
    Container(
      width: 300.0,
      color: Colors.pink,
      child: const Center(
          child: Text("600 Million",
              style: TextStyle(fontSize: 18, color: Colors.white))),
    ),
  ]),
  const SizedBox(height: 10.0),
  Row(children: [
    const SizedBox(
      width: 100.0,
      child: Text("Spanish"),
    ),
    Container(
      width: 280.0,
```

```
            color: Colors.cyan,
            child: const Center(
                child: Text("540 Million",
                    style: TextStyle(fontSize: 18, color: Colors.white))),
          ),
        ]),
        const SizedBox(height: 10.0),
        Row(children: [
          const SizedBox(
            width: 100.0,
            child: Text("Arabic"),
          ),
          Container(
            width: 140.0,
            color: Colors.deepPurple,
            child: const Center(
                child: Text("270 Million",
                    style: TextStyle(fontSize: 18, color: Colors.white))),
          ),
        ]),
      ]),
    )
  ],
);
}
}
```

Discussion

In the example code, the Column widget is used to build a bar chart interface that represents the top five spoken languages in the world as of the year 2022, as shown in Figure 9-9.

Figure 9-9. Column example output

The area defined for the column is defined as a SingleChildScrollView to ensure the screen remains responsive and will render correctly. Allocation of `height` and `width` properties are applied at the SizedBox widget per item and are used to constrain the area available within the Column widget.

When a constraint is applied within the UI, the widget will attempt to dynamically handle the changes presented. In some situations, the changes cannot be rendered correctly, which leads to an overflow error.

Overflows are a very common error and are displayed as a series of yellow and black stripes on-screen. Such an error is accompanied by an overflow warning indicating why the error occurred. To understand the options applicable to constraints, consult the Flutter documentation (*https://oreil.ly/Mo9ah*). In the example, a SingleChild-ScrollView widget is used to ensure the overflow error does not impact the code.

When using a Column widget, you can align content on the x-axis (horizontal) and y-axis (vertical). Alignment on the horizontal (x-axis) is enabled with `crossAxis Alignment`. Make use of this alignment to start content in a specific position on-screen, such as the `start`, `center`, or `end`.

Use the `mainAxisAlignment` property for alignment on the y-axis. Alignment ensures that the free space is evenly distributed between child elements, including before and after the first/last child in the array. The `mainAxisAlignment` also supports `start`, `center`, and `end` properties to shift the y-axis anchor.

Column and Row widgets share a lot of commonality. Reference Recipe 9.10 for a direct comparative with a Row widget.

9.10 Using a Row

Problem

You need a flexible widget to present as a horizontal layout on-screen.

Solution

Use a Row widget to allow its children widgets to be displayed as a horizontal array.

Here's an example of how to use the Row widget in Flutter to display information on-screen:

```
import 'package:flutter/material.dart';

void main() => runApp(const MyApp());

class MyApp extends StatelessWidget {
  const MyApp({Key? key}) : super(key: key);

  static const String _title = 'Example';

  @override
  Widget build(BuildContext context) {
    return const MaterialApp(
      title: _title,
      home: MyStatelessWidget(),
    );
  }
}

class MyStatelessWidget extends StatelessWidget {
  const MyStatelessWidget({Key? key}) : super(key: key);

  @override
  Widget build(BuildContext context) {
    return Scaffold(
      appBar: AppBar(title: const Text('Row Example')),
      body: _buildRowWidget(),
    );
  }

  Widget _buildRowWidget() {
    return Row(
```

```
        mainAxisAlignment: MainAxisAlignment.start,
        crossAxisAlignment: CrossAxisAlignment.end,
        children: [
          Container(
              width: 5,
              color: Colors.transparent,
          ),
          Expanded(
            child: Container(
              height: 50,
              width: 200,
              color: Colors.red,
              child: const Center(
                child: Text("50"),
              ),
            ),
          ),
          Expanded(
            child: Container(
              height: 100,
              width: 200,
              color: Colors.green,
              child: const Center(
                child: Text("100"),
              ),
            ),
          ),
          Expanded(
            child: Container(
              height: 200,
              width: 200,
              color: Colors.orange,
              child: const Center(
                child: Text("200"),
              ),
            ),
          ),
          Container(
              width: 5,
              color: Colors.transparent,
          ),
        ]);
    }
  }
```

Discussion

In the example code, data rows are created on the horizontal (x-axis), as shown in
Figure 9-10. Row widgets are static, meaning they do not have scrolling capability
without the use of an additional widget.

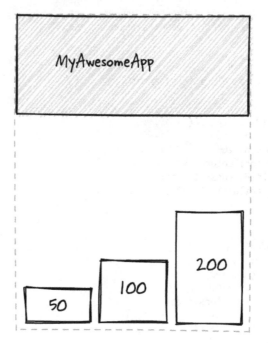

Figure 9-10. Row widget example

If the data displayed overflows beyond the screen dimensions, it is displayed as a series of yellow and black stripes on-screen. The example applies a constraint to the widget displayed, so it will dynamically adjust to the screen size. To understand the options applicable to constraints, consult the Flutter documentation (*https://oreil.ly/ Mo9ah*).

The alignment of the vertical (y-axis) uses the `mainAxisAlignment` property to use the start of the screen as an anchor. The `mainAxisAlignment` supports `start`, `center`, and `end` properties to shift the y-axis anchor.

Alignment on the horizontal (x-axis) is performed by `crossAxisAlignment`. Again, this method supports `start`, `center`, and `end` properties to shift the x-axis anchor.

Column and Row widgets share a lot of commonality. Reference Recipe 9.9 for a direct comparative with a Column widget.

9.11 Using an Expanded Widget

Problem

You want to automatically utilize any available on-screen space.

Solution

Use the Expanded widget to coordinate the available space visible to the user (i.e., the viewport).

Here's an example in which we use an Expanded widget to define three on-screen elements that will coordinate to use the available on-screen dimensions:

```dart
import 'package:flutter/material.dart';

void main() {
  runApp(const MyApp());
}

class MyApp extends StatelessWidget {
  const MyApp({Key? key}) : super(key: key);

  @override
  Widget build(BuildContext context) {
    const title = 'Expanded Widget';

    return MaterialApp(
      title: title,
      home: Scaffold(
        appBar: AppBar(
          title: const Text(title),
        ),
        body: const MyExpandedWidget(),
      ),
    );
  }
}

class MyExpandedWidget extends StatelessWidget {
  const MyExpandedWidget();

  @override
  Widget build(BuildContext context) {
    return Column(
      children: [
        Expanded(
          child: Container(
            color: Colors.red,
          ),
        ),
        Expanded(
          child: Container(
            color: Colors.transparent,
            child: Center(
              child: RichText(
                text: const TextSpan(
                  text: 'Luxembourg',
```

```
            style: TextStyle(
              fontWeight: FontWeight.bold,
              fontSize: 24,
              color: Colors.grey,
            ),
          ),
        ),
      ),
    )),
    Expanded(
      child: Container(
        color: Colors.blue,
      ),
    ),
  ],
  );
  }
}
```

Discussion

In the example code, the Expanded widget is used to recreate the flag of Luxembourg, as shown in Figure 9-11. The Expanded widget is enclosed within a Column widget, and each row is given an appropriate color.

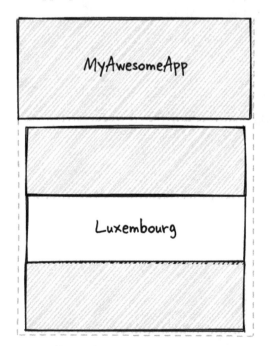

Figure 9-11. Expanded widget example

Despite the simplicity of the Expanded widget, it can be used in a variety of use cases. In the example, rather than perform a query on the dimensions on the screen, the Expanded widget is used to automatically fill the available space. Expanded (as the name suggests) will expand to the screen dimensions automatically. You do not have to specify the proportions; these will be calculated dynamically (i.e., responsively).

In a situation where your application will want to know how to ratio the viewport allocation between each item, an Expanded widget can be super useful. In this instance, the Expanded widget can be used to automatically provide the correct dimensions available within the viewport.

An example of where an Expanded widget's behavior can be beneficial is when you are working with Lists.

If you have a ListView widget and another on-screen widget and you wish to display both on-screen, you will need to make the widgets aware of how much of the viewport they can have. Reference the example in Figure 9-12, in which a ListView will attempt to fill the screen by default; if you don't want this behavior, you will need to use a widget to constrain the space to be allocated.

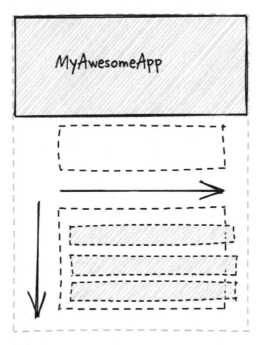

Figure 9-12. A ListView widget enclosed within an Expanded widget

Use the Expanded widget in conjunction with the ListView to tell it that it should only consume the remaining viewport (i.e., the user's visible area on-screen). Remember, widgets will typically look to their parents for guidance on constraints to be applied, such as `height` and `width`.

## CHAPTER 10

Developing User Interfaces

In this chapter, we move on to the topic of building user interfaces. Now that you have mastered the basics of Flutter widgets, the next step involves extending your knowledge to other key areas. The discussion focuses on the key technical elements of designing a beautiful interface. You will learn how to:

- Utilize fonts to enhance the text interface
- Define the on-screen layout for better placement
- Address identification of the host platform
- Leverage the features of Flutter to fundamentally improve your applications
- Understand how to address platform-specific areas of functionality through the Dart SDK
- Construct code that works with Flutter to present information in the most performant manner

Hopefully, the recipes incorporated in this chapter will allow you to take your development journey to the next level. Often, simple changes such as selection of fonts and the addition of responsiveness to your application make a huge difference to the overall impression. The recipes shown in this chapter will be key to building extensible applications to delight your users.

10.1 Using the Google Fonts Package

Problem

You want to use external fonts in a Flutter application.

Solution

Flutter allows you to incorporate external fonts as part of your application. If you are not sure how to add a fonts package, see Recipe 8.4.

Here's how to use Google Fonts (*https://fonts.google.com*) to display a custom font in a Flutter application:

```
import 'package:flutter/material.dart';
import 'package:google_fonts/google_fonts.dart';

void main() => runApp(MyApp());

class MyApp extends StatelessWidget {
  @override
  Widget build(BuildContext context) {
    return MaterialApp(
      title: 'Google Fonts Demo',
      debugShowCheckedModeBanner: false,
      theme: ThemeData(
          primarySwatch: Colors.blue,
          textTheme: TextTheme(
              bodyText1:
                  GoogleFonts.aBeeZee(fontSize: 30, color: Colors.deepOrange),
              bodyText2:
                  GoogleFonts.aBeeZee(fontSize: 30, color: Colors.white60))),
      home: const MyHomePage(title: 'Flutter and Dart Cookbook'),
    );
  }
}

class MyHomePage extends StatelessWidget {
  final String title;

  const MyHomePage({
    Key? key,
    required this.title,
  }) : super(key: key);

  @override
  Widget build(BuildContext context) {
    return Scaffold(
      backgroundColor: Colors.black,
      body: Column(children: [
        const Text('Yo MTV Raps'),
        Text(
          'Yo MTV Raps',
          style: GoogleFonts.coiny(fontSize: 30, color: Colors.blueGrey),
        ),
        Text(
          'Yo MTV Raps',
          style: GoogleFonts.actor(fontSize: 30, color: Colors.indigo),
```

```
      ),
    ]),
  );
}
```

Discussion

In the example, Google Fonts are used to demonstrate incorporating new typesetting within your application.

In the application, two approaches are used to set the Google Font. First, the text Theme is set as part of the general application theme. Use this approach if you want to set a default for your application. A common question is why the style bodyText2 takes precedence. The reason is this is set to the default text style for Material-themed applications.

The second approach applies the Google Font directly to the Text widget. Here we can individually set the font as required.

10.2 Incorporating RichText

Problem

You want to have more control over the text displayed on-screen.

Solution

Use the RichText widget to customize the text rendered on-screen. Here's how to use RichText to write custom text in a Flutter application:

```
import 'package:flutter/material.dart';

void main() {
  runApp(const MyApp());
}

class MyApp extends StatelessWidget {
  const MyApp({Key? key}) : super(key: key);

  @override
  Widget build(BuildContext context) {
    const title = 'RichText Demo';

    return MaterialApp(
      title: title,
      home: Scaffold(
        appBar: AppBar(
          title: const Text(title),
```

```
        ),
        body: const MyRichText(),
      ),
    );
  }
}

double screenHeight = 0.0;

class MyRichText extends StatelessWidget {
  const MyRichText({Key? key}) : super(key: key);

  @override
  Widget build(BuildContext context) {
    screenHeight = MediaQuery.of(context).size.height / 3;

    return RichText(
      text: const TextSpan(
        children: [
          TextSpan(
            text: 'Hello',
            style: TextStyle(fontWeight: FontWeight.bold, fontSize: 24),
          ),
          TextSpan(
            text: 'Luxembourg',
            style: TextStyle(
                fontWeight: FontWeight.bold, fontSize: 32, color: Colors.grey),
          ),
        ],
      ),
    );
  }
}
```

Discussion

In the example code, RichText is used to display information using two distinct styles. In the first instance, the text has a bold style applied. In the second, the text color is set to the color grey. The example code makes use of a media query, which is discussed in Recipe 10.6.

When you require greater control over how the application text will be rendered, use RichText. It will provide more control over the various styles that can be applied while still providing the functionality associated with a Text widget.

10.3 Identifying the Host Platform

Problem

You want to verify which platform the application is being run on to take account of the target platform.

Solution

In some instances you may wish to know the specific host platform the application is running on. This can be useful if you need to observe the user criteria to be applied within an application such as Android or iOS.

Here's how to check which host platform the application is running on:

```dart
import 'package:flutter/material.dart';
import 'dart:io' show Platform;
import 'package:flutter/foundation.dart' show kIsWeb;

void main() {
  runApp(const MyApp());
}

class MyApp extends StatelessWidget {
  const MyApp({Key? key}) : super(key: key);

  @override
  Widget build(BuildContext context) {
    const title = 'Platform demo';

    return MaterialApp(
      title: title,
      home: Scaffold(
        appBar: AppBar(
          title: const Text(title),
        ),
        body: const MyPlatformWidget(),
      ),
    );
  }
}

class MyPlatformWidget extends StatelessWidget {
  const MyPlatformWidget({Key? key}) : super(key: key);

  bool get isMobileDevice => !kIsWeb && (Platform.isIOS || Platform.isAndroid);
  bool get isDesktopDevice =>
      !kIsWeb && (Platform.isMacOS || Platform.isWindows || Platform.isLinux);
  bool get isMobileDeviceOrWeb => kIsWeb || isMobileDevice;
  bool get isDesktopDeviceOrWeb => kIsWeb || isDesktopDevice;
```

```
    bool get isAndroid => !kIsWeb && Platform.isAndroid;
    bool get isFuchsia => !kIsWeb && Platform.isFuchsia;
    bool get isIOS => !kIsWeb && Platform.isIOS;
    bool get isLinux => !kIsWeb && Platform.isLinux;
    bool get isMacOS => !kIsWeb && Platform.isMacOS;
    bool get isWindows => !kIsWeb && Platform.isWindows;

    @override
    Widget build(BuildContext context) {
      return Column(
        children: [
          Text(
            'isMobileDeviceOrWeb: $isMobileDeviceOrWeb',
            style: const TextStyle(fontSize: 20, color: Colors.grey),
          ),
          Text(
            'isDesktopDeviceOrWeb: $isDesktopDeviceOrWeb',
            style: const TextStyle(fontSize: 20, color: Colors.grey),
          ),
        ],
      );
    }
  }
```

Discussion

In the example code,[1] the Dart platform is interrogated to reference set values indicating the type of platform the application is being run on. Use *dart.io* to access the platform class, which has properties such as isMobileDevice or isLinux.

If you need to access this information in your application, import the *dart.io* package so that the necessary platform properties can be accessed. When you need to address the design constraints of a particular device type or understand where your application is being deployed, this package can be particularly helpful.

In addition, when testing it is useful to understand which host platform the application is running on. Flutter enables you to detect the host platform using predefined platform constants. In the documentation, the information relating to the host platform is located under device segmentation and referenced in the platform API.

The platform API supports the main platforms (i.e., Android, Fuchsia, iOS, Linux, macOS, and Windows). As part of the example, each test for a specific configuration can be used to identify the host platform. In addition, there is a separate setting (i.e., kIsWeb) for web-based applications.

---

1 At the time of writing, *dartpad.dev* does not support the use of *dart.io*.

10.4 Using a Placeholder Widget

Problem

You want to build a user interface when not all graphical assets are available.

Solution

Use the Placeholder widget to represent interface resources that have yet to be added to an application.

Here's an example where we revisit the Expanded widget code from Recipe 9.11. Instead of adding the necessary colors and text, a Placeholder widget is used:

```
import 'package:flutter/material.dart';

void main() {
  runApp(const MyApp());
}

class MyApp extends StatelessWidget {
  const MyApp({Key? key}) : super(key: key);

  @override
  Widget build(BuildContext context) {
    const title = 'Expanded Widget';

    return MaterialApp(
      title: title,
      home: Scaffold(
        appBar: AppBar(
          title: const Text(title),
        ),
        body: const MyExpandedWidget(),
      ),
    );
  }
}

class MyExpandedWidget extends StatelessWidget {
  const MyExpandedWidget();

  @override
  Widget build(BuildContext context) {
    return Column(
      children: const [
        Expanded(
          child: Placeholder(
              fallbackHeight: 400, strokeWidth: 10, color: Colors.red),
        ),
        Expanded(
```

```
          child: Placeholder(
              fallbackHeight: 400, strokeWidth: 10, color: Colors.white),
        ),
        Expanded(
          child: Placeholder(
              fallbackHeight: 400, strokeWidth: 10, color: Colors.blue),
        ),
      ],
    );
  }
}
```

Discussion

In the example code, the Placeholder widget is used to reserve a section of the display. The reservation enables you to continue development where artifacts such as images and text may not immediately be available. The result of adding a placeholder is a box with a cross outlining where the missing content should be rendered, as shown in Figure 10-1.

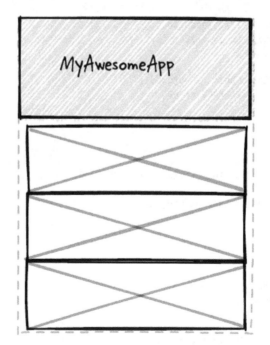

Figure 10-1. Placeholder widget example

The example code illustrates how a placeholder can be used to fill space that would otherwise be used when the required information is available. If you need to allocate visual space without necessarily needing to add the supporting resource, a Place-holder widget can be super helpful.

The Placeholder supports additional properties such as widget height (`fallback Height`) and width (`fallbackWidth`) to enable devices to scale gracefully. In addition, the widget also supports color (`color`) and line width (`strokeWidth`) to provide additional flexibility in the design stage of building an application.

10.5 Using a LayoutBuilder

Problem

You want to compose a layout based on the device context, e.g., portrait or touchscreen, in an adaptive manner.

Solution

Use a LayoutBuilder widget to handle the screen adaptive layout requirements automatically.

Here we revisit our flag example from RichText and display a number of columns relating to the width of the screen display:

```
import 'package:flutter/material.dart';

void main() => runApp(const MyApp());

class MyApp extends StatelessWidget {
  const MyApp({Key? key}) : super(key: key);

  static const String _title = 'LayoutBuilder';

  @override
  Widget build(BuildContext context) {
    return const MaterialApp(
      title: _title,
      home: MyStatelessWidget(),
    );
  }
}

class MyStatelessWidget extends StatelessWidget {
  const MyStatelessWidget({Key? key}) : super(key: key);

  @override
  Widget build(BuildContext context) {
    return Scaffold(
      appBar: AppBar(title: const Text('LayoutBuilder Example')),
      body: LayoutBuilder(
```

```dart
      builder: (BuildContext context, BoxConstraints constraints) {
        // Restrict based on Width
        if (constraints.maxWidth > 800) {
          return _buildTripleContainers();
        } else
        if (constraints.maxWidth > 600 && constraints.maxWidth<=800) {
          return _buildDoubleContainers();
        } else {
          return _buildSingleContainer();
        }
      },
    ),
  );
}

Widget _buildSingleContainer() {
  return Center(
    child: Container(
      height: 400.0,
      width: 100.0,
      color: Colors.red,
    ),
  );
}

Widget _buildDoubleContainers() {
  return Center(
    child: Row(
      mainAxisAlignment: MainAxisAlignment.spaceEvenly,
      children: <Widget>[
        Container(
          height: 400.0,
          width: 100.0,
          color: Colors.yellow,
        ),
        Container(
          height: 400.0,
          width: 100.0,
          color: Colors.yellow,
        ),

      ],
    ),
  );
}

Widget _buildTripleContainers() {
  return Center(
    child: Row(
      mainAxisAlignment: MainAxisAlignment.spaceEvenly,
      children: <Widget>[
        Container(
```

```
          height: 400.0,
          width: 100.0,
          color: Colors.green,
        ),
        Container(
          height: 400.0,
          width: 100.0,
          color: Colors.green,
        ),
        Container(
          height: 400.0,
          width: 100.0,
          color: Colors.green,
        ),
      ],
    ),
  );
}
}
```

Discussion

In the example code, the LayoutBuilder widget is used to return a specific view based on the screen dimensions available. The constraint applied is based on width and will track the size of the available window, returning a specific view when the set criterion is met. If the window is greater than 800 in width, you would see three green vertical rectangles. When the window width is between 600 and 800, you will see two yellow vertical rectangles. Otherwise, you will see a single red vertical rectangle. The three possible views are displayed in Figure 10-2.

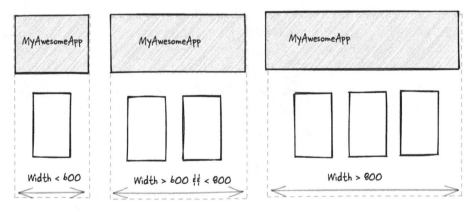

Figure 10-2. LayoutBuilder widget example

LayoutBuilder enables developers to adapt their application layout and can be used in situations where you need to understand how to compose the screen based on the available on-screen constraints.

The LayoutBuilder widget provides an adaptive interface; the most common scenario for this would be where an app runs on different devices. As devices have different dimensions, being able to dynamically render content within defined size constraints is super handy. The benefit associated with this moves beyond screen dimensions and includes the hardware to be interrogated, such as type of input (mouse and keyboard), visual density (web versus mobile), and selection type.

For each call to a LayoutBuilder widget, you are able to query the viewport dimensions via the BoxConstraints class associated with the view context. The typical use case for this functionality is to use the constraints structure to define viewport thresholds. These thresholds can be used to marshal the available dimensions in an efficient manner. Use LayoutBuilder to enable smart composition of screens to be displayed. An example using the device dimensions is one of many ways this widget can be used.

Contrast the LayoutBuilder widget with the MediaQuery class (Recipe 10.6), which takes into account the application size and orientation. The MediaQuery class provides information in relation to responsiveness (i.e., attuned to the available device settings), while LayoutBuilder provides an adaptive layout widget for composing on-screen elements (i.e., type of input, visual density, and selection type).

10.6 Accessing Screen Dimensions Using MediaQuery

Problem

You want to access the dimensions of a device.

Solution

Use the MediaQuery class to find information relating to the host device. The class will return a variety of properties distinct to the device, such as aspect ratio, padding, and orientation.

Here's an example where we use the MediaQuery class to return information about the host device and output information about the current environment settings:

```
import 'package:flutter/material.dart';

void main() {
  runApp(const MyApp());
}

class MyApp extends StatelessWidget {
  const MyApp({Key? key}) : super(key: key);

  @override
  Widget build(BuildContext context) {
    const title = 'MediaQuery demo';
```

```
    return MaterialApp(
      title: title,
      home: Scaffold(
        appBar: AppBar(
          title: const Text(title),
        ),
        body: const MyMediaQueryWidget(),
      ),
    );
  }
}

class MyMediaQueryWidget extends StatelessWidget {
  const MyMediaQueryWidget({Key? key}) : super(key: key);

  @override
  Widget build(BuildContext context) {
    var screenSize = MediaQuery.of(context).size;
    if (screenSize.width > 600) {
      // Two Column
      return Column(
        crossAxisAlignment: CrossAxisAlignment.start,
        children: [
          const Text(
            'You can Fit Two columns here!',
            style: TextStyle(fontSize: 30, color: Colors.grey),
          ),
          const SizedBox(height: 10.0),
          Text(
            'Screen Width: ${MediaQuery.of(context).size.width}',
            style: const TextStyle(fontSize: 20, color: Colors.grey),
          ),
          Text(
            'Screen Height: ${MediaQuery.of(context).size.height}',
            style: const TextStyle(fontSize: 20, color: Colors.grey),
          ),
          Text(
            'Aspect Ratio: ${MediaQuery.of(context).size.aspectRatio}',
            style: const TextStyle(fontSize: 20, color: Colors.grey),
          ),
          Text(
            'Orientation: ${MediaQuery.of(context).orientation}',
            style: const TextStyle(fontSize: 20, color: Colors.grey),
          ),
        ],
      );
    } else {
      return Column(
        crossAxisAlignment: CrossAxisAlignment.start,
        children: [
          const Text(
```

```
        'You can Fit One column here!',
        style: TextStyle(fontSize: 30, color: Colors.grey),
      ),
      const SizedBox(height: 10.0),
      Text(
        'Screen Width: ${MediaQuery.of(context).size.width}',
        style: const TextStyle(fontSize: 20, color: Colors.grey),
      ),
      Text(
        'Screen Height: ${MediaQuery.of(context).size.height}',
        style: const TextStyle(fontSize: 20, color: Colors.grey),
      ),
      Text(
        'Aspect Ratio: ${MediaQuery.of(context).size.aspectRatio}',
        style: const TextStyle(fontSize: 20, color: Colors.grey),
      ),
      Text(
        'Orientation: ${MediaQuery.of(context).orientation}',
        style: const TextStyle(fontSize: 20, color: Colors.grey),
      ),
    ],
  );
  }
 }
}
```

Discussion

As shown in Figure 10-3, in the example code the `MediaQuery` is used to return context-specific information relating to the device configuration. The context provides the `screenSize`, and this is used to display a different screen composition based on the width returned. `MediaQuery` is always available, so it is a very handy way to gather intelligence on how to access a variety of settings.

Invoking `MediaQuery.of`, as per the example, will mean a rebuild of the widget tree if the properties change. Therefore, when using this class be mindful of performance impact caused by the automatic rebuild whenever changes occur (e.g., device rotation, size update).

In the Flutter documentation (*https://oreil.ly/5PCU1*), a key distinction is the difference between responsiveness and adaptability. The bottom line is that responsiveness is attuned to the available screen size. If you intend to consider different device types, then you are more likely to want to incorporate adaptability (reference Recipe 10.5), e.g., mouse, keyboard, component selection strategy.

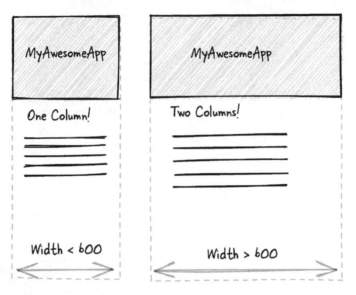

Figure 10-3. MediaQuery example

If you have ever worked with web development, you will most likely be familiar with MediaQuery. Typically, this class can be used to help provide properties used to assist in creating a responsive interface. Specifically, the MediaQuery.of(context) method can be used to access information such as the device orientation setting, textScale Factor state, padding applied, limitation applied to animation, and platform Brightness, indicating the contrast level.

## CHAPTER 11

Organizing On-Screen Data

In this chapter, we move to exploring how to define data on-screen. Fortunately, Flutter provides some very nice elements out of the box that are able to deal with presentation of information in a manageable way.

An important factor in developing Flutter applications is starting with the correct foundation. In many instances, how the code is laid out will bring forward both strengths and weaknesses. Understanding when to use particular techniques or data structures will most definitely increase your enjoyment and efficiency when building with Flutter.

To get started, we focus on the most common data use cases you will come across as a Flutter developer. You will learn how to:

- Build a vertical list
- Create a horizontal list
- Add a responsive header section
- Use a grid to display items
- Display a notification

The recipes cover a variety of use cases that will most certainly be very useful when building your application. For example, a vertical list is one of the most common design patterns in Flutter, so you will be in good company once you have learned how to use this.

When creating more complex applications, always try to make Dart and Flutter do the hard work. Each iteration of the language and framework delivers better efficiencies. Incorporating these new features (e.g., null safety) in each new release will help you to avoid certain errors and encourage better coding practice.

Given the flexibility of Flutter, don't forget that you can extend platform widgets (e.g., Text, Containers, etc.) as far as your imagination will take you. The recipes show you how to develop with the widgets, but where you take things beyond that is down to your skill and desire to build the next big thing.

11.1 Implementing a Vertical ListView

Problem

You want to incorporate a vertical list of items in a Flutter application.

Solution

In Flutter, a series of text items is typically rendered as a vertical list using the List-View widget. The ListView widget provides a simple mechanism for consolidating data to be rendered in a consistent format.

Here's an example of how to add a vertical ListView in a Flutter application:

```
import 'package:flutter/material.dart';

class ListTileItem {
  final String monthItem;

  const ListTileItem({
    required this.monthItem,
  });
}

class ListDataItems {
  final List<String> monthItems = [
    'January',
    'February',
    'March',
    'April',
    'May',
    'June',
    'July',
    'August',
    'September',
    'October',
    'November',
    'December',
  ];

  ListDataItems();
}

void main() {
  runApp(const MyApp());
```

```
    }

class MyApp extends StatelessWidget {
  const MyApp({Key? key}) : super(key: key);

  @override
  Widget build(BuildContext context) {
    const title = 'MyAwesomeApp';

    return MaterialApp(
      title: title,
      home: Scaffold(
        appBar: AppBar(
          title: const Text(title),
        ),
        body: MyListView(),
      ),
    );
  }
}

class MyListView extends StatelessWidget {
  MyListView();

  final ListDataItems item = ListDataItems();

  @override
  Widget build(BuildContext context) {
    return ListView.builder(
      itemCount: item.monthItems.length,
      itemBuilder: (context, index) {
        return ListTile(title: Text(item.monthItems[index]));
      },
    );
  }
}
```

Discussion

In the example, the code shown uses a separate data class to pass to a builder structure, which is then output as a ListView, as shown in Figure 11-1. Let's discuss each of these items in turn.

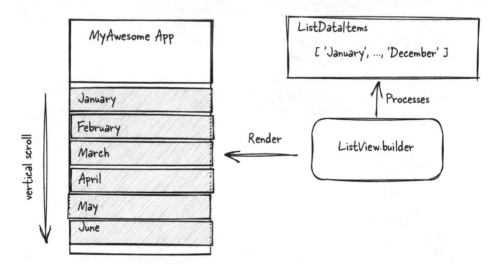

Figure 11-1. Vertical ListView example

The `ListDataItems` class is defined for the month information that will be ultimately displayed in our ListView widget. Observe how the class definition means we can treat the `ListDataItems` class in isolation. Reference Recipe 4.1 for information on how to use a List. Being able to amend data structures with minimal impact on the application functionality is a good approach to take. For example, if we add/delete a month item, we don't need to change any of the code that processes the `ListData Items` class.

Within the `MyListView` class, we declare a ListView builder. The builder is used to iterate through the `ListDataItems` structure. A combination of builder and ListView provides a memory-efficient method for managing large volumes of data to be rendered on-screen. While you can use a ListView without a builder, it is highly recommended to adopt the builder within your applications, as this approach is ultimately more scalable for handling lists of data.

For each item the `ListView.builder` processes, it calls the `ListTile` class and renders a Text widget that displays the name of the month. ListViews use the ListTile widget to show information, so this is another combination you will see when using a ListView.

By default, ListViews are vertical in nature; for information on how to create a horizontal list, see Recipe 11.2.

11.2 Implementing a Horizontal ListView

Problem

You want to incorporate a horizontal list of items in a Flutter application.

Solution

Creating a horizontal list can be performed in a manner similar to the way we create a vertical list (as done in Recipe 11.1). However, in most use cases, you also need to ensure the list created is able to react dynamically (i.e., height and width) based on the viewport to be displayed.

Here's an example of how to add a horizontal ListView in a Flutter application:

```
import 'package:flutter/material.dart';

class ListTileItem {
  final String monthItem;

  const ListTileItem({
    required this.monthItem,
  });
}

class ListDataItems {
  final List<String> monthItems = [
    'January',
    'February',
    'March',
    'April',
    'May',
    'June',
    'July',
    'August',
    'September',
    'October',
    'November',
    'December',
  ];

  ListDataItems();
}

void main() {
  runApp(const MyApp());
}

class MyApp extends StatelessWidget {
  const MyApp({Key? key}) : super(key: key);
```

```
    @override
    Widget build(BuildContext context) {
      const title = 'MyAwesomeApp';

      return MaterialApp(
        title: title,
        home: Scaffold(
          appBar: AppBar(
            title: const Text(title),
          ),
          body: MyListView(),
        ),
      );
    }
  }

  class MyListView extends StatelessWidget {
    MyListView({Key? key}) : super(key: key);
    final ListDataItems item = ListDataItems();

    @override
    Widget build(BuildContext context) {
      return ListView.builder(
        scrollDirection: Axis.horizontal,
        itemCount: item.monthItems.length,
        itemBuilder: (context, index) {
          return Row(
            crossAxisAlignment: CrossAxisAlignment.start,
            children: [
              Text(item.monthItems[index]),
              const SizedBox(
                width: 10.0,
              ),
            ],
          );
        },
      );
    }
  }
```

Discussion

In the example, the code shown uses a separate data class to pass to a builder structure, which is then output as a ListView, as shown in Figure 11-2. Let's discuss each of
these items in turn.

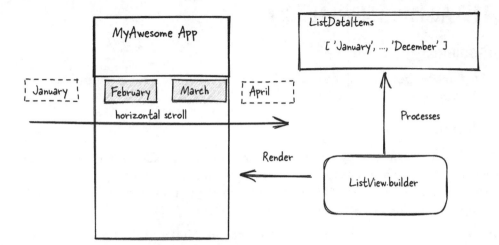

Figure 11-2. Horizontal ListView example

The `ListDataItems` class is defined for the month information that will be ultimately displayed in our ListView widget. Observe how the class definition means we can treat the `ListDataItems` class in isolation. Reference Recipe 4.1 for information on how to use a List. Being able to amend data structures with minimal impact on the application functionality is a good approach to take. For example, if we add/delete a month item, we don't need to change any of the code that processes the `ListData Items` class.

Within the `MyListView` class, we declare a ListView builder. The builder is used to iterate through the `ListDataItems` structure. A combination of builder and ListView provides a memory-efficient method for managing large volumes of data to be rendered on-screen. As mentioned in Recipe 11.1 you can use a ListView without a builder, but it is highly recommended to adopt the builder within your applications, as this approach is ultimately more scalable for handling lists of data.

For each item the `ListView.builder` processes, a Row widget item is declared and used to render information on-screen. As part of the `ListView.builder`, we also add some initialization for the data. First we tell the ListView that we want the data to be rendered on `Axis.horizontal`, meaning we want a horizontal list. Remember, the default for a ListView is a vertical list. Next, we add some formatting to the Row widget (see Recipe 9.10) to indicate where the data should be output. Use the Row `crossAxisAlignment` property to tell the application where you wish the item to be placed. The final part of the rendering is to add a SizedBox (see Recipe 9.8) to apply a spacer to the information to be output.

For information on how to create a vertical ListView, see Recipe 11.1.

11.3 Adding a SliverAppBar

Problem

You want to create a responsive header for an application based on user scrolling activity.

Solution

Use the SliverAppBar widget to build a responsive header for your application. The default setting for a SliverAppBar is to not show the app bar until the top of the list is present. Add the property SliverAppBar(floating: true,) to make the AppBar reappear when the user scrolls up the screen.

Here's an example of how to add a SliverAppBar in a Flutter application:

```
import 'package:flutter/material.dart';


void main() => runApp(MyApp());

class MyApp extends StatelessWidget {
  @override
  Widget build(BuildContext context) {
    return MaterialApp(
      title: 'SliverAppBar Demo',
      debugShowCheckedModeBanner: false,
      theme: ThemeData(
        primarySwatch: Colors.blue,
      ),
      home: const MyHomePage(title: 'Flutter and Dart Cookbook'),
    );
  }
}

class MyHomePage extends StatelessWidget {
  final String title;

  const MyHomePage({
    Key? key,
    required this.title,
  }) : super(key: key);

  @override
  Widget build(BuildContext context) {
    return Scaffold(
      backgroundColor: Colors.grey[300],
      body: const CustomScrollView(
        slivers: [
          SliverAppBar(
```

```
            leading: Icon(Icons.menu),
            title: Text('Sliver App Bar'),
            expandedHeight: 300,
            collapsedHeight: 150,
            floating: false,
          ),
        ], // End
      ),
    );
  }
}
```

Discussion

In the example, the code shown adds a SliverAppBar widget to the application. Before using this particular widget, you may wish to review the widget discussion on Scaffold (see Recipe 9.4) and AppBar (Recipe 9.5).

The SliverAppBar widget provides a responsive AppBar that reacts to the scroll context of an application.

In Figure 11-3, we observe two specific behaviors from the SliverAppBar widget. When a user scrolls toward the bottom of the screen, the AppBar reacts by reducing the AppBar size. The impact of this is to provide more room to view the items displayed below the header area. When a user scrolls back to the top of the screen, the action is reversed, and as the user gets closer to the top, the AppBar returns to the original size. A point to note is that the Scaffold AppBar property is removed in the example and replaced by SliverAppBar within the body property.

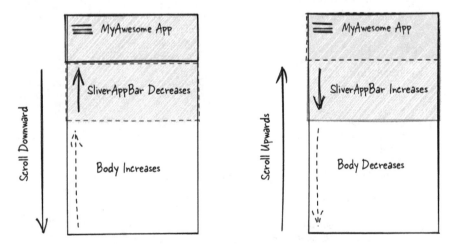

Figure 11-3. SliverAppBar example

Control of the dimensions of the SliverAppBar are provided by the properties `expandedHeight: 300` and `collapsedHeight: 150`. Both properties are customizable, meaning you as developer control the on-screen representation.

When using a SliverAppBar widget, use a SliverList (see Recipe 11.4) rather than a ListView widget to process information. A SliverList is designed to cooperate with the SliverAppBar and will ensure better compatibility within your application.

11.4 Adding a SliverList

Problem

You want to include a list to work with a dynamic SliverAppBar header based on user scrolling activity.

Solution

Use a SliverList when working with the SliverAppBar header. A SliverAppBar includes custom data processing to assist with the scrolling aspect of the header and data interaction.

Here's an example of how to add a SliverList in a Flutter application:

```
import 'package:flutter/material.dart';

class CarItem {
  final String title;
  final String subtitle;
  final String url;

  CarItem({
    required this.title,
    required this.subtitle,
    required this.url,
  });
}

class ListDataItems {
    final List<CarItem> carItems = [
    CarItem(
        title: '911 Cabriolet',
        subtitle: '911 Carrera Cabriolet Porsche',
        url:
            'https://oreil.ly/m3OXC'),
    CarItem(
        title: '718 Spyder',
        subtitle: '718 Spyder Porsche',
        url:
            'https://oreil.ly/hca-6'),
    CarItem(
        title: '718 Boxster T',
        subtitle: '718 Boxster T Porsche',
```

```
            url:
                'https://oreil.ly/Ws4EX'),
        CarItem(
            title: 'Cayenne',
            subtitle: 'Cayenne S Porsche',
            url:
                'https://oreil.ly/gwvnL'),
        CarItem(
            title: '911 Cabriolet',
            subtitle: '911 Carrera Cabriolet Porsche',
            url:
                'https://oreil.ly/m30XC'),
        CarItem(
            title: '718 Spyder',
            subtitle: '718 Spyder Porsche',
            url:
                'https://oreil.ly/hca-6'),
        CarItem(
            title: '718 Boxster T',
            subtitle: '718 Boxster T Porsche',
            url:
                'https://oreil.ly/Ws4EX'),
        CarItem(
            title: 'Cayenne',
            subtitle: 'Cayenne S Porsche',
            url:
                'https://oreil.ly/gwvnL'),
        CarItem(
            title: '911 Cabriolet',
            subtitle: '911 Carrera Cabriolet Porsche',
            url:
                'https://oreil.ly/m30XC'),
        CarItem(
            title: '718 Spyder',
            subtitle: '718 Spyder Porsche',
            url:
                'https://oreil.ly/hca-6'),
        CarItem(
            title: '718 Boxster T',
            subtitle: '718 Boxster T Porsche',
            url:
                'https://oreil.ly/Ws4EX'),
        CarItem(
            title: 'Cayenne',
            subtitle: 'Cayenne S Porsche',
            url:
                'https://oreil.ly/gwvnL'),
    ];

  ListDataItems();
}

void main() => runApp(MyApp());

class MyApp extends StatelessWidget {
  @override
  Widget build(BuildContext context) {
```

```
    return MaterialApp(
      title: 'SliverList Widget Demo',
      debugShowCheckedModeBanner: false,
      theme: ThemeData(
        primarySwatch: Colors.blue,
      ),
      home: const MyHomePage(title: 'Flutter and Dart Cookbook'),
    );
  }
}

class MyHomePage extends StatelessWidget {
  final String title;

  const MyHomePage({
    Key? key,
    required this.title,
  }) : super(key: key);

  @override
  Widget build(BuildContext context) {
    return Scaffold(
      backgroundColor: Colors.grey[300],
      body: CustomScrollView(
        slivers: [
          const SliverAppBar(
            leading: Icon(Icons.menu),
            title: Text('MyAwesomeApp'),
            expandedHeight: 300,
            collapsedHeight: 150,
            floating: false,
          ),
          // Next, create a SliverList
          MySliverList(),
        ], // End
      ),
    );
  }
}

class MySliverList extends StatelessWidget {
  MySliverList({ Key? key }) : super(key: key);

  final ListDataItems item = ListDataItems();

  @override
  Widget build(BuildContext context) {
    return // Next, create a SliverList
        SliverList(
      // Use a delegate to build items as they're scrolled on-screen.
      delegate: SliverChildBuilderDelegate(
        (context, index) => ListTile(
        leading: CircleAvatar(
          backgroundImage: NetworkImage(item.carItems[index].url),
        ),
        title: Text(item.carItems[index].title),
        subtitle: Text(item.carItems[index].subtitle),
```

```
        ),
            // Builds 1000 ListTiles
            childCount: item.carItems.length,
        ),
    );
    }
}
```

Discussion

In the example, the code adds a SliverList to process information combined with a SliverAppBar. Before using this particular widget, you may wish to review the Sliver-AppBar widget discussion (see Recipe 11.3). The SliverList widget works in tandem with a SliverAppBar widget, providing a reactive interface to user scroll interactivity.

In Figure 11-4, as the user scrolls down the screen, they are presented with more list items. In unison, the SliverAppBar header shrinks and takes up less screen space. As the user scrolls up the screen, the SliverAppBar grows as they get closer to the top of the screen.

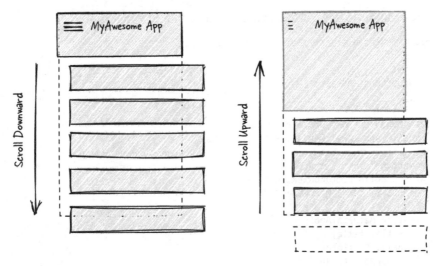

Figure 11-4. SliverList example

The SliverList is passed an item count, and this is used to determine how many iterations are used by the widget. SliverChildBuilderDelegate is used to process the information to be displayed on-screen. The processing mechanism is similar to a ListView.builder and expects a data structure based on a List. Ensure the child Count property is set to the length of the list to be processed, to display all associated information. Remember that Lists provide a length property, so this information is available to us without any additional work.

With that, your SliverList is ready to process data, and you can pass it a List-based data structure. As we have learned across multiple chapters, the information to be presented on-screen will be based on a widget, so organize the data as required. In the example code, as we are using a List, a ListTile is used, displaying an icon together with some Text widget values.

11.5 Adding a GridView of Items

Problem

You want a way to show information as a grid of items.

Solution

Use a GridView when you want to structure data to use both horizontal and vertical layout. A GridView combines horizontal and vertical distribution of data based on the available screen dimensions.

Here's an example of how to add a GridView in a Flutter application:

```
import 'package:flutter/material.dart';

void main() {
  runApp(const MyApp());
}

class MyApp extends StatelessWidget {
  const MyApp({Key? key}) : super(key: key);

  @override
  Widget build(BuildContext context) {
    const title = 'MyAwesomeApp';

    return MaterialApp(
      title: title,
      home: Scaffold(
        appBar: AppBar(
          title: const Text(title),
        ),
        body: const MyGridViewBuilderWidget(),
      ),
    );
  }
}

class MyGridViewBuilderWidget extends StatelessWidget {
  const MyGridViewBuilderWidget({Key? key}) : super(key: key);
  final gridItems = 10;
```

```
@override
Widget build(BuildContext context) {
  return GridView.builder(
      itemCount: gridItems,
      gridDelegate:
          const SliverGridDelegateWithFixedCrossAxisCount(crossAxisCount: 5),
      itemBuilder: (context, index) {
        return Padding(
            padding: const EdgeInsets.all(8.0),
            child: Container(
              height: 50,
              width: 50,
              color: Colors.blue,
              child: Center(child: Text(index.toString())),
            ));
      });
  }
}
```

Discussion

In the example, a GridView widget is used to display a series of blue boxes containing a Text representing the positional index value. Use a GridView as an alternative to a ListView (see Recipes 11.1 and 11.2).

In Figure 11-5, note that a GridView automatically wraps content visible on the screen. The example includes an index, so you can that see the default direction used by a GridView is horizontal. The item on which the GridView wraps is set by the property crossAxisCount, which is set to 5 in the code. Also note that since the default direction is horizontal, content will continue being added horizontally until it either completes the list or needs to wrap on the vertical axis.

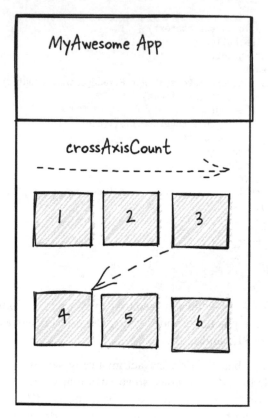

Figure 11-5. GridView example

The GridView is derived from a CustomScrollView with a single SliverGrid. When adding items, you will see it uses a SliverGridDelegateWithFixedCrossAxisCount, allowing us to control the number of items on the horizontal axis. Similar to other builder methods, we need to provide an indication of how many items are to be processed via the `itemCount` property. If you are passing in a List, note the `itemCount` should be set to `List.length`.

An alternative to using `GridView.builder` is using `GridView.count` to manually process the items within the grid. Realistically, it is easier to just learn to use a builder method for even the most simple use cases, as it provides a more flexible approach. Processing one or two items is not a very common use case and requires you to write significantly more code to perform the same task.

11.6 Adding a SnackBar (Pop-up Notification)

Problem

You want a way to display a short-lived notification to the user.

Solution

Use a SnackBar widget to display a temporary on-screen notification. The notification will be linked to an event within your application, such as a user tapping an item.

Here's an example of how to add a SnackBar widget in a Flutter application:

```
import 'package:flutter/material.dart';

void main() {
  runApp(const MyApp());
}

class MyApp extends StatelessWidget {
  const MyApp({Key? key}) : super(key: key);

  @override
  Widget build(BuildContext context) {
    const title = 'MyAwesomeApp';

    return MaterialApp(
      title: title,
      home: Scaffold(
        appBar: AppBar(
          title: const Text(title),
        ),
        body: MyListView(),
      ),
    );
  }
}

class ListViewData {
  final List<String> monthItems = [
    'January',
    'February',
    'March',
  ];
}

class MyListView extends StatelessWidget {
  MyListView({Key? key}) : super(key: key);

  final ListViewData items = ListViewData();
```

```
  @override
  Widget build(BuildContext context) {
    return ListView.builder(
        itemCount: items.monthItems.length,
        itemBuilder: (context, index) {
          return ListTile(
            title: Text(items.monthItems[index]),
            onTap: () {
              ScaffoldMessenger.of(context).showSnackBar(
                SnackBar(
                  content: Text('You selected ${items.monthItems[index]}'),
                ),
              );
            },
          );
        });
  }
}
```

Discussion

A SnackBar is useful when you need to indicate an activity has been performed—for example, indicating a button has been tapped or a file has been downloaded.

In Figure 11-6, when the user taps on the month displayed on-screen, a notification will briefly appear at the bottom of the screen. The notification in the example is linked to the ListTile widget; therefore, it will respond with a message indicating which month was tapped by the user.

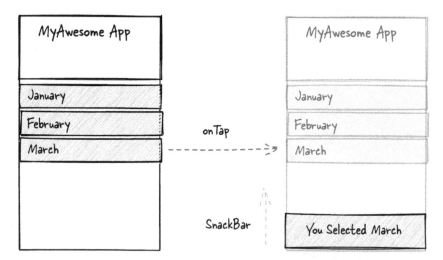

Figure 11-6. SnackBar widget example

The SnackBar widget provides a notification back to the user. You can override the default settings of the SnackBar as desired. For example, the default duration of four seconds can be overridden by introducing the following code:

```
SnackBar(
  duration: const Duration(seconds: 10, milliseconds: 500),
  content: Text('You selected $listTitle'),
),
```

In addition to providing feedback to the user, the SnackBar can also perform additional actions. Extend the SnackBar definition to include a label and a gesture to initiate a complementary action:

```
SnackBar(
  action: SnackBarAction(
    label: 'action',
    onPressed: () {},

  ),
  duration: const Duration(seconds: 10, milliseconds: 500),
  content: Text('You selected $listTitle'),
),
```

You can utilize this feature to invoke additional activities similar to those seen with the more common menu-based options.

## CHAPTER 12

Flutter Page Navigation

In this chapter, we look at how to perform common page navigation techniques. Page navigation is a very common use case for developers. Fortunately, Flutter makes much of this interface building easy for us.

So far the discussion has focused on building an application with a single page. However, you will now likely want to expand beyond this base case to allow navigation between multiple pages. To get started, we focus on common navigation patterns you will come across as a Flutter developer. You will learn how to:

- Use routes to move between pages
- Add a navigation draw widget
- Add a tab interface widget
- Add a bottom navigation widget
- Pass data using keys

Being able to move between pages using in-built navigation will make your applications look more professional. Flutter provides a number of ways to navigate between information pages, so it is worth knowing how to incorporate these into your own applications. By the end of this chapter you will have covered the basics of general page navigation using routes.

12.1 Adding Page Navigation with Routes (Imperative)

Problem

You want a way to move between multiple pages using specific navigational instructions.

Solution

Use Flutter navigation. Flutter navigation uses routes, which provide the mechanism to traverse between pages. A route refers to the address of the page to be accessed. Routing between pages requires the use of a MaterialPageRoute, which is used to push a new page on the application stack, replacing the current page.

Here's an example of how to perform navigation between two distinct pages:

```dart
import 'package:flutter/material.dart';

void main() {
  runApp(MyApp());
}

class MyApp extends StatelessWidget {
  MyApp({Key? key}) : super(key: key);

  final List<String> items = [
    'January',
    'February',
    'March',
    'April',
    'May',
    'June',
    'July',
    'August',
    'September',
    'October',
    'November',
    'December'
  ];

  @override
  Widget build(BuildContext context) {
    const title = 'MyAwesomeApp';

    return MaterialApp(
      title: title,
      home: Scaffold(
        appBar: AppBar(
          title: const Text(title),
        ),
        body: ListView.builder(
          itemCount: items.length,
          itemBuilder: (context, index) {
            return MyListView(items[index]);
          },
        ),
      ),
    );
  }
```

```
    }

class MyListView extends StatelessWidget {
  const MyListView(this.title);

  final String title;

  @override
  Widget build(BuildContext context) {
    return ListTile(
      title: Text(title),
      onTap: () {
        Navigator.push(
          context,
          MaterialPageRoute(
            builder: (context) => MyDetails(title),
          ),
        );
      },
    );
  }
}

class MyDetails extends StatelessWidget {
  const MyDetails(this.itemTitle);

  final String itemTitle;

  @override
  Widget build(BuildContext context) {
    const title = 'Details Page';

    return Scaffold(
      appBar: AppBar(
        title: const Text(title),
      ),
      body: SafeArea(
        top: false,
        bottom: false,
        child: Padding(
          padding: const EdgeInsets.all(8.0),
          child: Column(
            children: [
              SizedBox(
                height: 338.0,
                width: 800.0,
                child: Card(
                  clipBehavior: Clip.antiAlias,
                  child: Column(
                    crossAxisAlignment: CrossAxisAlignment.start,
                    children: [
                      // Divider(),
```

```
              Padding(
                padding: const EdgeInsets.all(10.0),
                child: Text(itemTitle),
              )
            ],
          ),
        ),
      ),
    ],
  ),
),
),
);
}
}
```

Discussion

In the example, an onTap event is set up per ListTile, meaning that when we select an individual item in the List, an event will be generated. The event is associated with a Navigator.push to request a new page be displayed.

When using Navigator V1 with imperative routing, traversal is much simplified. The imperative navigation mechanism uses a stack to push and pop the relevant page navigation, allowing you to move between pages. In Figure 12-1, navigation between pages is explicitly stated by using the MaterialPageRoute.

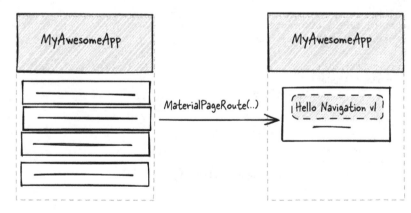

Figure 12-1. MaterialPageRoute class example

Using the MaterialApp will automatically create the navigation icons required. In this instance, the back arrow is shown on the details screen without any additional coding. Ensure the Scaffold widget definition added to the Details Page does not redefine the MaterialApp.

`Navigator.push` implements a stack mechanism where new screens are added and removed as the user navigates between them. The routing between screens is handled automatically, so you as a developer just need to indicate the page to be used within the current build context. When returning from the new page, the application will initiate the pop mechanism to move to the previous page:

```
onTap: () {
  Navigator.push(
    context,
    MaterialPageRoute(
      builder: (context) => MyDetails(title),
    ),
  );
},
```

The declarative (Navigator V2) routing provides a more sophisticated mechanism that keeps track of navigation state. In this mode, you can think of Flutter behaving similarly to web page navigation. An approach such as this allows you to jump between links and dynamically keep track of placement.

12.2 Adding Page Navigation with Routes (Declarative)

Problem

You want a way to navigate to a defined page path based on an established routing workflow of an application.

Solution

Use Flutter navigation. Flutter navigation allows developers to define the routes to be used, creating a declarative approach for moving between screens. Take this approach when you need to follow a defined workflow that has a defined flow to be applied, e.g., a sign-up process.

Here's an example of how to use declarative routing between multiple pages following a defined workflow:

```
import 'package:flutter/material.dart';

void main() => runApp(const MyApp());

class MyApp extends StatelessWidget {
  const MyApp({super.key});

  @override
  Widget build(BuildContext context) {
    return MaterialApp(
      title: 'Flutter Code Sample for Navigator',
```

```
      // MaterialApp contains our top-level Navigator
      initialRoute: '/signup',
      routes: <String, WidgetBuilder>{
        '/': (BuildContext context) => const HomePage(),
        '/signup': (BuildContext context) => const SignUpPage(),
      },
    );
  }
}

class HomePage extends StatelessWidget {
  const HomePage({super.key});

  @override
  Widget build(BuildContext context) {
    return DefaultTextStyle(
      style: Theme.of(context).textTheme.headline4!,
      child: Container(
        color: Colors.white,
        alignment: Alignment.center,
        child: const Text('Home Page'),
      ),
    );
  }
}

class SignUpPage extends StatelessWidget {
  const SignUpPage({super.key});

  @override
  Widget build(BuildContext context) {
    // SignUpPage builds its own Navigator, which ends up being a nested
    // Navigator in our app.
    return Navigator(
      initialRoute: 'signup/personal_info',
      onGenerateRoute: (RouteSettings settings) {
        WidgetBuilder builder;
        switch (settings.name) {
          case 'signup/personal_info':
            // Assume CollectPersonalInfoPage collects personal info and then
            // navigates to 'signup/choose_credentials'.
            builder = (BuildContext context) => const CollectPersonalInfoPage();
            break;
          case 'signup/choose_credentials':
            // Assume ChooseCredentialsPage collects new credentials and then
            // invokes 'onSignupComplete()'.
            builder = (BuildContext _) => ChooseCredentialsPage(
                  onSignupComplete: () {
                    // Referencing Navigator.of(context) from here refers to the
                    // top-level Navigator because SignUpPage is above the
                    // nested Navigator that it created. Therefore, this pop()
                    // will pop the entire "sign-up" journey and return to the
```

```dart
                // "" route, AKA HomePage.
                Navigator.of(context).pop();
              },
            );
          break;
        default:
          throw Exception('Invalid route: ${settings.name}');
      }
      return MaterialPageRoute<void>(builder: builder, settings: settings);
    },
  );
  }
}

class ChooseCredentialsPage extends StatelessWidget {
  const ChooseCredentialsPage({
    super.key,
    required this.onSignupComplete,
  });

  final VoidCallback onSignupComplete;

  @override
  Widget build(BuildContext context) {
    return GestureDetector(
      onTap: onSignupComplete,
      child: DefaultTextStyle(
        style: Theme.of(context).textTheme.headline4!,
        child: Container(
          color: Colors.pinkAccent,
          alignment: Alignment.center,
          child: const Text('Choose Credentials Page'),
        ),
      ),
    );
  }
}

class CollectPersonalInfoPage extends StatelessWidget {
  const CollectPersonalInfoPage({super.key});

  @override
  Widget build(BuildContext context) {
    return DefaultTextStyle(
      style: Theme.of(context).textTheme.headline4!,
      child: Container(
        color: Colors.white,
        child: Column(
        crossAxisAlignment: CrossAxisAlignment.start,
        children: [
          const Text(
            "Name: Max, Address: Fury Road",
```

```
              style: TextStyle(fontSize: 20, color: Colors.black87),
            ),
            const SizedBox(height: 10.0),
            GestureDetector(
              onTap: () {
                // This moves from the personal info page to the credentials page,
                // replacing this page with that one.
                Navigator.of(context)
                    .pushReplacementNamed('signup/choose_credentials');
              },
              child: const SizedBox(
                child: Text(
                  'Link: Page',
                  style: TextStyle(
                      fontSize: 20,
                      color: Colors.blue,
                      decoration: TextDecoration.underline),
                ),
              ),
            ),
          ],
        ),
      ),
    );
  }
}
```

Discussion

In the example, the application is defined to follow a designated path for the user when accessing the application, as shown in Figure 12-2.

The example uses three distinct screens to mock the user journey associated with entering information, checking credentials, and finally accessing the application home screen. In order to progress to the next screen, a condition needs to be met. If the user is unable to meet that condition, then they are unable to navigate to the next screen.

The application features Navigator-defined routes. With this approach, the screen navigation is more predictable for link-based traversal. While the implementation is more complex than Navigator V1 (see Recipe 12.1), it does provide greater flexibility for routing within an application.

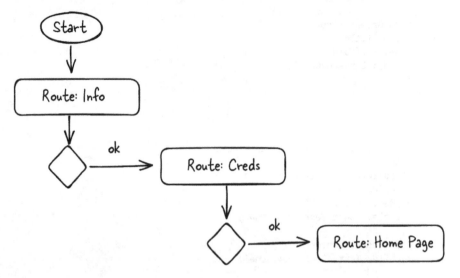

Figure 12-2. Navigator V2 routing example

12.3 Implementing a Navigation Drawer

Problem

You want a way to create an off-screen navigation menu.

Solution

Use the Drawer widget to host a series of navigation points. The Drawer widget can be thought of as a menu featuring suboptions. In the example code, you will use three different options set up to perform navigation. Adding a Drawer to your application provides a simple mechanism for navigating between options.

Here's an example of using a navigation drawer to provide access to a menu used to route directly to application information off-screen:

```dart
import 'package:flutter/material.dart';

void main() {
  runApp(const MyApp());
}

class MyApp extends StatelessWidget {
  const MyApp({Key? key}) : super(key: key);

  @override
  Widget build(BuildContext context) {
    const title = 'Drawer demo';
```

```dart
    return MaterialApp(
      title: title,
      home: Scaffold(
        body: DemoPageOne(),
      ),
    );
  }
}

class DemoPageOne extends StatelessWidget {
  @override
  Widget build(BuildContext context) {
    return Scaffold(
      appBar: AppBar(
        title: const Text("Page One"),
      ),
      body: const Center(
        child: Text('Demo: Page One'),
      ),
      drawer: const MyDrawerWidget(),
    );
  }
}

class DemoPageTwo extends StatelessWidget {
  @override
  Widget build(BuildContext context) {
    return Scaffold(
      appBar: AppBar(
        title: const Text("Page Two"),
      ),
      body: const Center(
        child: Text('Demo: Page Two'),
      ),
      drawer: const MyDrawerWidget(),
    );
  }
}

class DemoPageThree extends StatelessWidget {
  @override
  Widget build(BuildContext context) {
    return Scaffold(
      appBar: AppBar(
        title: const Text("Page Three"),
      ),
      body: const Center(
        child: Text('Demo: Page Three'),
      ),
      drawer: const MyDrawerWidget(),
    );
```

```
    }
  }

class DemoPageFour extends StatelessWidget {
  @override
  Widget build(BuildContext context) {
    return Scaffold(
      appBar: AppBar(
        title: const Text("Page Four"),
      ),
      body: const Center(
        child: Text('Demo: Page Four'),
      ),
      endDrawer: const MyDrawerWidget(),
    );
  }
}

class MyDrawerWidget extends StatelessWidget {
  const MyDrawerWidget({Key? key}) : super(key: key);

  @override
  Widget build(BuildContext context) {
    return Drawer(
      child: ListView(
        children: [
          const DrawerHeader(
            child: Icon(Icons.home, size: 35),
          ),
          ListTile(
            leading: const Icon(Icons.home),
            title: const Text('Drawer Item #1'),
            onTap: () {
              Navigator.of(context).push(
                MaterialPageRoute(builder: (context) => DemoPageOne()),
              );
            },
          ),
          ListTile(
            leading: const Icon(Icons.info),
            title: const Text('Drawer Item #2'),
            onTap: () {
              Navigator.of(context).push(
                MaterialPageRoute(builder: (context) => DemoPageTwo()),
              );
            },
          ),
          ListTile(
              leading: const Icon(Icons.favorite),
              title: const Text('Drawer Item #3'),
              onTap: () {
                Navigator.of(context).push(
```

```
                  MaterialPageRoute(builder: (context) => DemoPageThree()),
                );
              }),
          ListTile(
            leading: const Icon(Icons.list),
            title: const Text('Drawer Item #4'),
            onTap: () {
              Navigator.of(context).push(
                MaterialPageRoute(builder: (context) => DemoPageFour()),
              );
            }),
        ],
      ),
    );
  }
}
```

Discussion

In the example, the application defines a drawer that contains four items representing separate pages within the Flutter application. Selecting a drawer item will navigate the user to the page relating to the menu option.

An implementation of a Drawer widget includes a number of elements. The use case for a Drawer is typically where an application has been partitioned into a number of routes (i.e., pages, as shown in Figure 12-3).

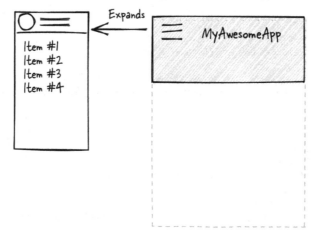

Figure 12-3. Drawer widget example

The drawer header (i.e., DrawerHeader) is used to hold information associated with the application. By convention, this can be set to an image such as an avatar representing the user or text:

```
const DrawerHeader(
  child: Icon(Icons.home, size: 35),
),
```

Typically, the drawer will open on the left-hand side; however, this is configurable by the developer. Drawers can be set to use either the left- or right-hand side of the screen as the anchor point. Use the Scaffold endDrawer property to amend the default left-hand side positioning of the drawer and open from the right-hand side of the screen:

```
return Scaffold(
  appBar: AppBar(
    title: const Text("Page Four"),
  ),
  body: const Center(
    child: Text('Demo: Page Four'),
  ),
  endDrawer: const MyDrawerWidget(),
);
```

View the code for DemoPageFour to see this in action. When using this page, also note that the Scaffold widget automatically handles the navigation to the previous page.

The selection of the page may be separate from the information displayed on the page. For example, the drawer contains a series of items relating to the page to be selected. Each menu item will invoke a specific page route featuring content specific to that item.

In the example, the drawer also utilizes a ListView with ListTile children to show the available options. Each ListTile calls a separate function to render the on-screen view. Within the ListTile, you will note that an icon, title, and subtitle are supported to provide visual feedback to the user. To ensure each item is selectable by the user, a gesture detector is added. Adding an onTap functionality can be combined with navigation to route to a specific page:

```
ListTile(
  leading: const Icon(Icons.list),
  title: const Text('Drawer Item #4'),
  onTap: () {
    Navigator.of(context).push(
      MaterialPageRoute(builder: (context) => DemoPageFour()),
    );
  }),
```

Adding drawer navigation to your application does not require too much effort, but do be mindful that this navigation does not suit every occasion. If you require hierarchical navigation (e.g., page 1 goes to page 2 and then to page 3), consider an alternative method of routing between pages.

12.4 Working with Tabs

Problem

You want to use tabs to show different content.

Solution

Use a TabBar to display multiple pages separated by defined categories.

Here's an example in which a TabBar widget is used to display information for different items relating to a fictitious financial services application:

```dart
import 'package:flutter/material.dart';

void main() => runApp(MyApp());

class MyApp extends StatelessWidget {
  @override
  Widget build(BuildContext context) {
    return MaterialApp(
      title: 'Flutter and Dart Cookbook Demo',
      debugShowCheckedModeBanner: false,
      theme: ThemeData(
        tabBarTheme: const TabBarTheme(
          labelColor: Colors.white,
          labelStyle: TextStyle(color: Colors.grey),
// color for text
        ),
        primarySwatch: Colors.blue,
      ),
      home: const MyHomePage(title: 'Flutter and Dart Cookbook'),
    );
  }
}

class MyHomePage extends StatelessWidget {
  final String title;

  const MyHomePage({
    Key? key,
    required this.title,
  }) : super(key: key);

  @override
  Widget build(BuildContext context) {
    return Scaffold(
      backgroundColor: Colors.black,
      body: DefaultTabController(
        length: 4,
        child: Scaffold(
```

```
      appBar: AppBar(
        title: const Text('MyAwesomeTabBar'),
        bottom: const TabBar(
//           indicatorColor: Colors.black,
          tabs: [
            Tab(
              icon: Icon(Icons.home, color: Colors.white),
              child: Text('Home',
                  style: TextStyle(fontWeight: FontWeight.bold)),
            ),
            Tab(
              icon: Icon(Icons.account_balance, color: Colors.white),
              child: Text('Account',
                  style: TextStyle(fontWeight: FontWeight.bold)),
            ),
            Tab(
              icon: Icon(Icons.calculate, color: Colors.white),
              child: Text('Payments',
                  style: TextStyle(fontWeight: FontWeight.bold)),
            ),
            Tab(
              icon: Icon(Icons.credit_score, color: Colors.white),
              child: Text('Card',
                  style: TextStyle(fontWeight: FontWeight.bold)),
            ),
          ],
        ),
      ),
      body: const TabBarView(
        children: [
          SizedBox(
            child: Center(
              child: Text('Home Page Tab 1'),
            ),
          ),
          SizedBox(
            child: Center(
              child: Text('Account Page Tab 2'),
            ),
          ),
          SizedBox(
            child: Center(
              child: Text('Payments Page Tab 3'),
            ),
          ),
          SizedBox(
            child: Center(
              child: Text('Card Page Tab 4'),
            ),
          ),
        ],
      ),
```

```
      ),
    ),
  );
}
}
```

Discussion

In the example, the application defines multiple tab pages, each associated with an individual page. Selecting the tab item will switch focus to the appropriate pages linked to the active tab.

The typical use case for a TabBar is to show page information. In this scenario, each page has an icon/text to indicate the nature of the information shown, as depicted in Figure 12-4.

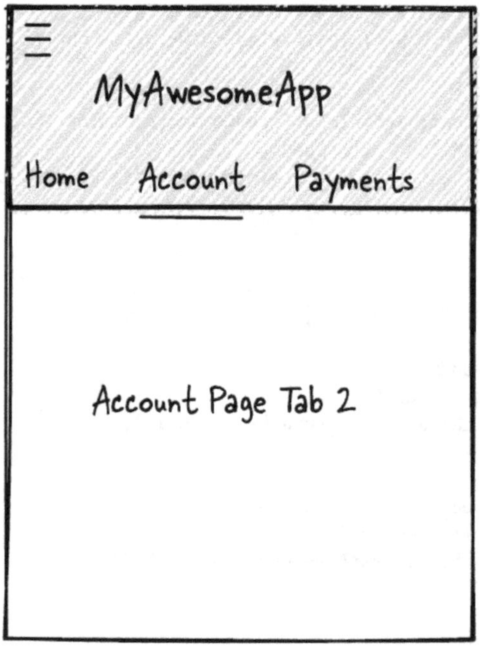

Figure 12-4. TabBar and TabBarView widget example

The default color of the TabView can be influenced by the ThemeData settings. Add a tabBarTheme setting to enable an updated color scheme to be used. For example, to change the label color, add a labelColor setting.

The TabBar colors at an individual level can also be changed by applying a color at the Tab level:

```
return MaterialApp(
  title: 'Flutter and Dart Cookbook Demo',
  debugShowCheckedModeBanner: false,
  theme: ThemeData(
    tabBarTheme: const TabBarTheme(
      labelColor: Colors.white,
    ),
    primarySwatch: Colors.blue,
  ),
  home: const MyHomePage(title: 'Flutter and Dart Cookbook'),
);
```

In the example code, both approaches have been used to illustrate how this works. In the example, observe how the TabBar is linked to the AppBar bottom property. Doing this will render the TabBar at the bottom of the application header.

In addition to a TabBar, a TabBarView can be used to display tab-specific content. To include content below the TabBar, incorporate this widget into the body property. Ensure there is the same number of TabBarViews declared as there are of the TabBar widget. As each tab is selected, the corresponding view will be displayed, filling the available viewport.

12.5 Adding a Bottom Navigation Bar

Problem

You want to provide user navigation at the bottom of the screen.

Solution

Use a bottom navigation widget to provide a common design element, usually based on icons.

Here's an example that demonstrates how to integrate this solution within your Flutter application:

```
import 'package:flutter/material.dart';

void main() {
  runApp(const MyApp());
}

class MyApp extends StatelessWidget {
  const MyApp({Key? key}) : super(key: key);

  @override
  Widget build(BuildContext context) {
    return const MaterialApp(
        title: "Bottom Navigation Widget", home: MyBottomNavigationWidget());
```

```dart
    }
  }

final List<Widget> _navigationPages = [
  const Center(child: Text('Page: Home')),
  const Center(child: Text('Page: News')),
  const Center(child: Text('Demo: Favorites')),
  const Center(child: Text('Demo: List')),
];

class MyBottomNavigationWidget extends StatefulWidget {
  const MyBottomNavigationWidget({Key? key}) : super(key: key);

  @override
  State<MyBottomNavigationWidget> createState() => _MyBottomNavigationWidget();
}

class _MyBottomNavigationWidget extends State<MyBottomNavigationWidget> {
  final appTitle = 'Bottom Navigation Widget';
  int _itemSelected = 0;

  void _bottomBarNavigation(int index) {
    setState(() {
      _itemSelected = index;
    });
  }

  @override
  Widget build(BuildContext context) {
    return Scaffold(
      appBar: AppBar(
        title: Text(appTitle),
      ),
      body: _navigationPages[_itemSelected],
      bottomNavigationBar: BottomNavigationBar(
        currentIndex: _itemSelected,
        onTap: _bottomBarNavigation,
        type: BottomNavigationBarType.fixed,
        items: const [
          BottomNavigationBarItem(icon: Icon(Icons.home), label: 'Home'),
          BottomNavigationBarItem(icon: Icon(Icons.info), label: 'News'),
          BottomNavigationBarItem(
              icon: Icon(Icons.favorite), label: 'Favorites'),
          BottomNavigationBarItem(icon: Icon(Icons.list), label: 'List'),
        ],
      ),
    );
  }
}
```

Discussion

In this example, we use a stateful widget to retain the state of the widget. In this case, it will store the selected `BottomNavigationBarItem`. Figure 12-5 shows a navigation bar where the code will display a distinct page for each item in the bottom navigation bar selected.

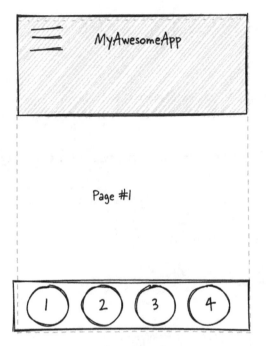

Figure 12-5. BottomNavigationBar widget example

When using a bottom navigation bar, each menu item can be made to perform a specific action when clicked. In the example app, a page with the title of the item selected is displayed. A stateful widget is integral to implementation, as it is used to hold the value of the current menu item. When the user selects an item, the code calls set state to update to the current selection (i.e., the property `currentIndex` set to the value of `_itemSelected`).

The type of navigation bar can be defined in a couple of ways. `Fixed` is the default setting and provides a consistent equidistant render of each icon on-screen. Set the `type` property to indicate what configuration to apply—e.g., `type: BottomNativa tionBarType.fixed`. Using this option means you are asking Flutter to handle the management of icon placement of four or fewer items. If you decide to use the `shifting` option, this means the icons are placed based on your criteria and provide a nice fade animation when using this option.

One common way to use a bottom navigation bar is to represent different views on-screen. If each navigation item is a different page, this expands the general application real estate. As the user selects a navigation icon, they are directed to the appropriate page to be displayed. Be mindful of using this with more complex scenarios featuring a hierarchy. While this option does offer a simple way to view data, adding many items (e.g., more than five) can quickly become confusing.

12.6 Using Keys to Pass Information

Problem

You want a way to pass information between widgets.

Solution

Use keys to pass information between stateful widgets. Keys are typically used to pass state as a key/value pair.

Here's an example to demonstrate information passing using keys and named parameters:

```
import 'package:flutter/material.dart';

void main() {
  runApp(const MyApp());
}

class MyApp extends StatelessWidget {
  const MyApp({Key? key}) : super(key: key);

  @override
  Widget build(BuildContext context) {
    const paramTitle = 'My Title';
    const paramName  = 'My Name';

    return MaterialApp(
      title: paramTitle,
      home: Scaffold(
        appBar: AppBar(
          title: const Text(paramTitle),
        ),
        body: const MyTextWidget(name:paramName, title:paramTitle),
      ),
    );
  }
}

class MyTextWidget extends StatelessWidget {
  final String title;
```

```
    final String name;
    const MyTextWidget({Key ?key, required this.title, required this.name})
      : super(key: key);

    @override
    Widget build(BuildContext context) {
      return Center(
        child: Text("$title $name"),
      );
    }
  }
```

Discussion

In this example, we use keys to pass information between the parent class and the child. As shown in Figure 12-6, there are two pieces of information to be sent to the MyTextWidget class.

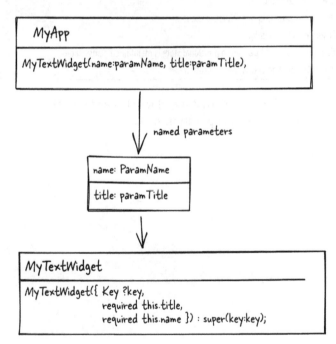

Figure 12-6. Key passing information example

Keys provide a simple mechanism to pass information and assist rendering of the correct state. To achieve this, a key/value pair is used that needs to be uniquely addressable. At a high level, subclasses should use either LocalKey or GlobalKey.

A local key is constrained by its parent, meaning it should be used in conjunction with elements to pass data. LocalKey is typically used when passing information via the elements within the widget tree.

A global key requires uniqueness across the application, meaning it cannot be duplicated. In a situation where it is impractical to coordinate a local key, use the global key to manage the desired state. To learn more about the use of keys in Flutter, I highly recommend watching the Flutter Widgets 101 episode "When to Use Keys (*https://youtu.be/kn0EOS-ZiIc*)" from the Flutter team.

Key can be used for more than preserving state and passing information between classes. There are a number of options that can be used for key types in Flutter:

Key	Purpose
Local	Distinguish between children
Value	Use the value of the key
Object	Use an object to uniquely reference the item
Unique	Ensure each key is unique
PageStorageKey	Hold the user scroll location, so positional state is maintained across pages
Global	Access information across the application

When using a stateful object, note that the global key extends the type state and thus provides access to the associated application state.

## CHAPTER 13

Handling Data Assets

In this chapter, you will learn how Flutter and Dart combine to manage data resources. Over the course of the chapter, you will see how the location of the data affects the approach to accessing the required information. Throughout this chapter, follow the recipes to learn various techniques to incorporate embedded, asset-based, and remote data into your application.

So far in this book, our examples have focused on data that is included directly in the application code. When you are using embedded data in this way, much of the preparatory work will have been done for you. Over the course of this chapter, we will look at processing JavaScript Object Notation (JSON), which is one of the most common formats used for ingesting data.

You will learn how to:

- Refactor data for an application
- Consume information from a local JSON file
- Work with data located in an assets folder
- Handle remote data consumption using a `Future`
- Automate JSON to a Dart class

We will be using two example JSON files to demonstrate how to load external data during this chapter. The format of each file is shown in the following samples:

- Sample 1: Single-layer JSON

  ```
  {
      "1": "January",
      "2": "February",
      "3": "March",
  ```

```
        "4": "April"
    }
```
- Sample 2: Multilayer JSON
```
{
    "data": [
        {
            "title": "January"
        },
        {
            "title": "February"
        },
        {
            "title": "March"
        }
    ]
}
```

Accessing external data is a very powerful technique to include within an application. Hopefully you will see that, once the data is loaded, the working practices developed over the previous chapters will remain relevant.

13.1 Accessing Data Strategically

Problem

You have data available but are unsure where it should be located.

Solution

Consider how the data will be used in the application, and apply the relevant strategy to efficiently access information. When working out the correct location for your data, consider:

- The volume of data to be stored
- The frequency of updates

Discussion

Within your application, data will be provided via a data pipeline that is responsible for loading information in a timely manner.

In Figure 13-1, three common data access patterns are outlined, based on where the application data will be located. During the development process, handling data assets will be essential to building more advanced applications. Data comes in many forms, and learning to utilize these data assets will be a useful skill to develop.

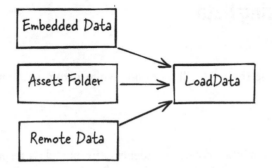

Figure 13-1. Data pipeline

Embedded/local data represents data colocated with the application. Remember that if you bundle data with an application, you need to include a method separate to an application update to replace the required dataset. Use embedded data where you have a large dataset or data that does not need to be updated on a frequent basis.

Assets folder data is often used for smaller datasets that provide initial functionality without requiring the user to perform an initial download. Loading data from the assets folder is a good approach where data does not require frequent updates and can therefore be bundled with the application. Holding data locally is not always advantageous. A key issue is ensuring the local data held doesn't become stale. One way to minimize stale data is to override the local assets folder data, e.g., apply a date or refresh cycle to the data held in the assets folder. If you don't do this, remember to incorporate a way to include new data when your application is updated. The bottom line is that holding data locally in an assets folder can be a quick way to organize data so that it is accessible. A typical use case for this functionality is holding data that is not time sensitive.

Remote data access is a strategy that many applications adopt. Remote data provides a lot of flexibility in that it is isolated from the application, so it can be changed independently. However, avoid associating significant dataset downloads with remote data, as this can be susceptible to error, leaving the application in an unworkable state. In addition, asynchronous code used to handle indeterminate function call duration will be used to access the data objects. When loading datasets, always consider using asynchronous rather than synchronous code to provide a better user experience.

Once you have the data available, another consideration is the frequency at which it will need to be refreshed. Again, consider the size of the dataset. A large dataset does not lend itself to frequent over-the-air updates. If your situation requires a large dataset, you will need to design an appropriate mechanism to handle data updates based on your requirement.

13.2 Refactoring Data

Problem

You want to increase the readability of code when using data embedded within an application.

Solution

To increase code readability, create an independent data class responsible for storing your data. Separating data into its own class makes it easier to extend the processing of data. We use a separate MyData class to provide two specific benefits—of isolation and abstraction. The two use cases are discussed in more detail below.

Here's an example in which the data to be processed resides within a class called MyData:

```
import 'package:flutter/material.dart';

void main() {
    runApp(MyApp());
}

class MyData {
    final List<String> items = [
    'January',
    'February',
    'March',
    'April',
    'May',
    'June',
    'July',
    'August',
    'September',
    'October',
    'November',
    'December'
  ];

  MyData();
}

class MyApp extends StatelessWidget {
  MyApp({Key? key}) : super(key: key);
  final MyData data = MyData();

  @override
  Widget build(BuildContext context) {
```

```
      const title = 'MyAwesomeApp';
      List items = data.items;

      return MaterialApp(
        title: title,
        home: Scaffold(
          appBar: AppBar(
            title: const Text(title),
          ),
          body: ListView.builder(
            itemCount: items.length,
            itemBuilder: (context, index) {
              return ListTile(
                title: Text(items[index]),
              );
            },
          ),
        ),
      );
    }
  }
```

Discussion

The MyData class definition is responsible for the declaration of data to be accessed in the application. The variable data is based on the MyData class. Access to the underlying data is performed by declaring a variable data of type MyData, which is responsible for accessing the information associated with the MyData class.

In the example, we create a new class called MyData. As outlined earlier, we do this to take advantage of data isolation and abstraction.

Isolation of data improves general readability of your code. By creating a class dedicated to holding our information, we can more easily understand the code. The MyData class is used to hold a List of strings. As the data definition and the data use are separate, our program is easier to read, as we can distinctly see the responsibility of each section of code.

Abstraction of data presents an opportunity to simplify the contract between use and implementation. In the example, to use the data class, we merely declare a reference to it. When we create an instance variable, that represents the object containing the data structure defined in the MyData class. At this point we don't know much about the implementation other than that it provides the required data. As an application becomes more complex, it is useful to be able to abstract definitions. In the preceding example, we have moved our data to a specific class and can extend this data class to perform additional actions as required.

13.3 Generating Dart Classes from JSON

Problem

You want to generate custom Dart classes without needing to write annotations or learning JSON serialization.

Solution

Use one of the many open source utilities, such as JSON to Dart Online Converter (*https://jsontodart.com*) or JSON to Dart (*https://oreil.ly/gR-gr*). The utility will define the classes required to transpose your JSON data.

Here are some example classes generated that demonstrate the output when using the Sample 2 JSON dataset:

```dart
class Month {
  List<Data>? data;

  Month({this.data});

  Month.fromJson(Map<String, dynamic> json) {
    if (json['data'] != null) {
      data = <Data>[];
      json['data'].forEach((v) {
        data!.add(new Data.fromJson(v));
      });
    }
  }

  Map<String, dynamic> toJson() {
    final Map<String, dynamic> data = new Map<String, dynamic>();
    if (this.data != null) {
      data['data'] = this.data!.map((v) => v.toJson()).toList();
    }
    return data;
  }
}

class Data {
  String? title;

  Data({this.title});

  Data.fromJson(Map<String, dynamic> json) {
    title = json['title'];
  }

  Map<String, dynamic> toJson() {
    final Map<String, dynamic> data = new Map<String, dynamic>();
```

```
      data['title'] = this.title;
      return data;
    }
  }
```

Discussion

As shown in Figure 13-2, we use an external tool to generate a series of Dart classes for consuming a JSON file. The sample classes were generated by the JSON to Dart site (*https://oreil.ly/gR-gr*) and are based on the Sample 2 JSON dataset. Add the class name of Month to generate a similar example to the preceding.

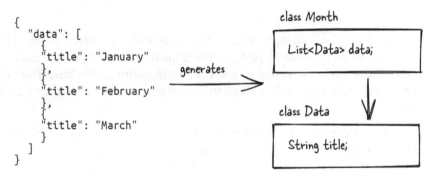

Figure 13-2. JSON to class example

At first glance the generated code may seem quite intimidating; however, in reality we just need to update three settings to meet our application requirements and the latest Dart best practices:

- Dart will likely point out to you that there is an "unnecessary new keyword" in your code. Dart made the use of the keyword new optional, so you can safely remove it where the compiler complains about it being in your code:

```
Month.fromJson(Map<String, dynamic> json) {
  if (json['data'] != null) {
    data = <Data>[];
    json['data'].forEach((v) {
      data!.add(new Data.fromJson(v));
    });
  }
}
```

- You may come across the delightful message "Use collection literals when possible." In your code, you need to update Map<String, dynamic>() to <String, dynamic>{} to remove this message and make the compiler happy once more:

```
Map<String, dynamic> toJson() {
  final Map<String, dynamic> data = Map<String, dynamic>();
  if (this.data != null) {
```

```
        data['data'] = this.data!.map((v) => v.toJson()).toList();
      }
      return data;
    }
```

- The last message relates to the use of the this keyword. If you see "Don't access members with `this` unless avoiding shadowing," then it's telling you to remove this reference from a variable, as it is not required:

```
Map<String, dynamic> toJson() {
  final Map<String, dynamic> data = <String, dynamic>{};
  data['title'] = this.title;
  return data;
}
```

Once you have made these changes, your Dart class is ready to be used in your Flutter application. While it's possible to perform the transition from JSON manually, it is more efficient and less error prone to use a utility to perform this task. The typical use case for this type of approach is when there will not be many changes required to the dataset.

Using an automated solution to transpose JSON can be more efficient where you need a quick render of a JSON dataset. If you have a more complex data structure it can be even more useful, as you no longer need to decipher the appropriate structure to use. Use a tool like this to dynamically read and process the desired structure.

13.4 Using Local JSON Data Asynchronously

Problem

You want a way to consume a string containing JSON information.

Solution

Use the inbuilt JSON processing capability of Dart to parse information formatted as JSON. Without the use of a package, processing Dart can be complex.

Here's an example, using the Sample 2 dataset of embedded JSON data. The JSON data is loaded asynchronously, allocated to a variable, and transposed to a string:

```
import 'package:flutter/material.dart';
import 'dart:convert';

void main() {
    runApp(MyApp());
}

// Example 2: JSON Dataset
class MyData {
```

```
    final String items = '{"data": [
      { "title": "January" },
      { "title": "February" },
      { "title": "March" },
      ] }';
}

class DataSeries {
  final List<DataItem> dataModel;

  DataSeries({required this.dataModel});

  factory DataSeries.fromJson(Map<String, dynamic> json) {
    var list = json['data'] as List;

    List<DataItem> dataList = list.map((dataModel) =>
    DataItem.fromJson(dataModel)).toList();

    return DataSeries(dataModel: dataList);
  }
}

class DataItem {
  final String title;

  DataItem({required this.title});

  factory DataItem.fromJson(Map<String, dynamic> json) {
    return DataItem(title: json['title']);
  }
}

class MyApp extends StatelessWidget {
  // This widget is the root of your application.
  @override
  Widget build(BuildContext context) {
    return MaterialApp(
      title: 'Local JSON Future Demo',
      theme: ThemeData(
        primarySwatch: Colors.blue,
      ),
      home: const MyHomePage(
        title: 'Local JSON Future Demo',
        key: null,
      ),
    );
  }
}

class MyHomePage extends StatefulWidget {
  const MyHomePage({Key? key, required this.title}) : super(key: key);
```

```dart
  final String title;

  @override
  State<MyHomePage> createState() => _MyHomePageState();
}

Future<String> _loadLocalData() async {
  final MyData data = MyData();

  return data.items;
}

class _MyHomePageState extends State<MyHomePage> {
  Future<DataSeries> fetchData() async {
    String jsonString = await _loadLocalData();
    final jsonResponse = json.decode(jsonString);
    DataSeries dataSeries = DataSeries.fromJson(jsonResponse);
    print(dataSeries.dataModel[0].title);

    return dataSeries;
  }

  late Future<DataSeries> dataSeries;

  @override
  void initState() {
    super.initState();
    dataSeries = fetchData();
  }

  @override
  Widget build(BuildContext context) {
    return Scaffold(
      appBar: AppBar(
        title: Text(widget.title),
      ),
      body: FutureBuilder<DataSeries>(
          future: dataSeries,
          builder: (context, snapshot) {
            if (snapshot.hasData) {
              return ListView.builder(
                itemCount: snapshot.data!.dataModel.length,
                itemBuilder: (BuildContext context, int index) {
                  return ListTile(
                    title: Text(snapshot.data!.dataModel[index].title),
                  );
                },
              );
            } else if (snapshot.hasError) {
              return Text("Error: ${snapshot.error}");
            }
            return const CircularProgressIndicator();
```

```
            }),
        );
    }
}
```

Discussion

In the example, the code introduces the use of `initState` and a `FutureBuilder`. The `initState` is a method used to perform tasks in the initialization phase of a class. Use this method to load assets prior to their use in an application, as per Figure 13-3. On completion of this phase, the data structure should be loaded with the local embedded data.

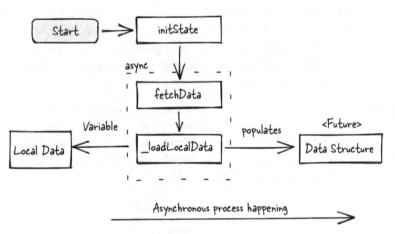

Figure 13-3. Load embedded data example

The call to `initState` is a one-off call, associated with the initialization of the `_My HomePageState`. During this method, make a call to `fetchData`, which is a generic async method used to load and process the data ready for use in the application. We use this method to reference the loading of data and also the processing of the information returned—in this instance, turning a JSON object into a String to be displayed in a ListView.

To transpose our input data from a JSON dataset, we use the imported *dart:convert* package. The package includes `json.decode`, which takes a string input and returns JSON.

 We do this step for the purpose of demonstration, as we will turn this information back into a String. Now we have the data transposed to JSON, and we can use the application library to manipulate the data into a List structure. The final step is to map the data into a `DataSeries` construct.

To load our data, we use a private method named _loadLocalData.

 This method is also asynchronous and marked as private, and just returns the value of our data structure containing our embedded JSON. The method is marked as private to indicate it is to be used internally with the class and is not for public access. It is this method that is used to determine the data to be loaded.

A FutureBuilder is yet another builder method to help you efficiently process data. If the asynchronous process has not completed, the FutureBuilder is intelligent enough to wait. The FutureBuilder will wait for the availability of our data; however, during that period, it will show a progress indicator to indicate a background action is occurring. Once the data is available, the FutureBuilder will display the data retrieved from the fetchData method. At that point the data loading process has completed, and the FutureBuilder will render the information based on the associated widget tree, as shown in Figure 13-4.

In our application, the FutureBuilder uses a dataset marked as a Future. A Future is an asynchronous call that improves the user experience when accessing data by offloading the effort from the main thread. Dart guidelines indicate that we should always use an asynchronous call for long-duration activities such as file reads, database queries, and the fetching of web page results.

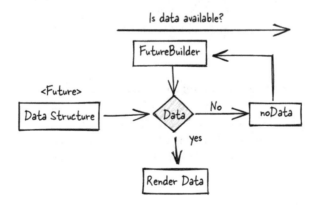

Figure 13-4. Embedded data rendering example

The Figure 13-4 illustrations represent a very common data loading pattern that you can use with large datasets. Remember the flow of the diagram and which aspects need to be defined as asynchronous.

13.5 Consuming a JSON Dataset from the Assets Folder

Problem

You want to use a custom assets folder to host a file to be programmatically consumed as input data.

Solution

Use the assets folder to host information to be loaded in your application. The assets folder represents a general-purpose storage for your application.

Update the *pubspec.yaml* to reference the *assets/example2.json* directory created:

```
flutter:
  uses-material-design: true
  assets:
    - assets/example2.json
```

Here's an example of how to access a JSON dataset located in the assets folder of your application:

```
import 'package:flutter/material.dart';
import 'dart:convert';

void main() {
    runApp(MyApp());
}

class DataSeries {
  final List<DataItem> dataModel;

  DataSeries({required this.dataModel});

  factory DataSeries.fromJson(Map<String, dynamic> json) {
    var list = json['data'] as List;

    List<DataItem> dataList = list.map((dataModel) =>
    DataItem.fromJson(dataModel)).toList();

    return DataSeries(dataModel: dataList);
  }
}

class DataItem {
  final String title;

  DataItem({required this.title});

  factory DataItem.fromJson(Map<String, dynamic> json) {
    return DataItem(title: json['title']);
```

```dart
  }
}

class MyApp extends StatelessWidget {
  // This widget is the root of your application.
  @override
  Widget build(BuildContext context) {
    return MaterialApp(
      title: 'JSON Future Demo',
      theme: ThemeData(
        primarySwatch: Colors.blue,
      ),
      home: const MyHomePage(
        title: 'JSON Future Demo',
        key: null,
      ),
    );
  }
}

class MyHomePage extends StatefulWidget {
  const MyHomePage({Key? key, required this.title}) : super(key: key);

  final String title;

  @override
  State<MyHomePage> createState() => _MyHomePageState();
}

Future<String> _loadAssetData() async {
  final AssetBundle rootBundle = _initRootBundle();
  return await rootBundle.loadString('assets/example2.json');
}

class _MyHomePageState extends State<MyHomePage> {
  Future<DataSeries> fetchData() async {
    String jsonString = await _loadAssetData();
    final jsonResponse = json.decode(jsonString);
    DataSeries dataSeries = DataSeries.fromJson(jsonResponse);
    print(dataSeries.dataModel[0].title);

    return dataSeries;
  }

  late Future<DataSeries> dataSeries;

  @override
  void initState() {
    super.initState();
    dataSeries = fetchData();
  }
```

```
    @override
    Widget build(BuildContext context) {
      return Scaffold(
        appBar: AppBar(
          title: Text(widget.title),
        ),
        body: FutureBuilder<DataSeries>(
            future: dataSeries,
            builder: (context, snapshot) {
              if (snapshot.hasData) {
                return ListView.builder(
                  itemCount: snapshot.data!.dataModel.length,
                  itemBuilder: (BuildContext context, int index) {
                    return ListTile(
                      title: Text(snapshot.data!.dataModel[index].title),
                    );
                  },
                );
              } else if (snapshot.hasError) {
                return Text("Error: ${snapshot.error}");
              }
              return const CircularProgressIndicator();
            }),
      );
    }
  }
```

Discussion

In the example, the code follows the pattern outlined in Recipe 13.3. The notable difference is that a `_loadAssetData` method is introduced, and this is used to access data hosted in the application assets folder.

 If you are using DartPad (*https://dartpad.dev*), be aware that unfortunately this site does not currently support loading local assets.

Figure 13-5 illustrates how the load process for assets works in Flutter. To load data from the assets folder, you need to reference the `rootBundle`. The `rootBundle` contains the resources that were bundled with the application when built. Any asset added within the assets subsection of the *pubspec.yaml* will be accessible via this property.

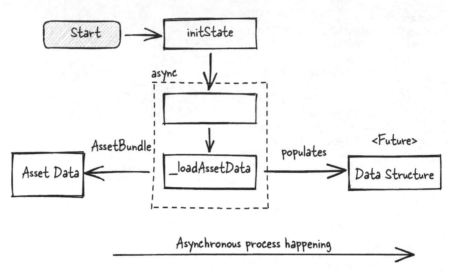

Figure 13-5. Assets data loading example

Resources for the Flutter application are stored in the `AssetBundle`. Resources added to the assets folder within the Flutter *pubspec.yaml* (see Recipe 8.1) are accessible via this property. To access the information in your application, create a `rootBundle` variable of type `AssetBundle`. From that `rootBundle` variable, you then have access to the assets declared in your application:

```
final AssetBundle rootBundle = _initRootBundle();
return await rootBundle.loadString('assets/example2.json');
```

If you choose to use an alternative structure within your assets folder, be sure to include the full path to the object you wish to load.

Once the folder and data are available, update the *pubspec.yaml*. Adding information to the (local) assets folder is a good way to store application data without needing to refer to an external solution such as a database or an API.

13.6 Accessing Remote JSON Data

Problem

You want to consume information from an external remote API.

Solution

Use the Dart *HTTP* package to access remote data sources. The package enables you to access and retrieve externally hosted information and use it via your application.

Here's an example that adds the *JSON* and *async* packages used to access remote data:

```dart
import 'package:http/http.dart' as http;
import 'dart:async' show Future;
import 'dart:convert';


Future<String> _loadRemoteData() async {
  final response = await (http
      .get(Uri.parse('https://oreil.ly/ndCPN')));
  if (response.statusCode == 200) {
    print('response statusCode is 200');
    return response.body;
  } else {
    print('Http Error: ${response.statusCode}!');
    throw Exception('Invalid data source.');
  }
}
```

Discussion

In the example, the code follows the pattern outlined in Recipe 13.3. The notable difference is that an `async` `_loadRemoteData` method, shown in Figure 13-6, is used to access data from the internet.

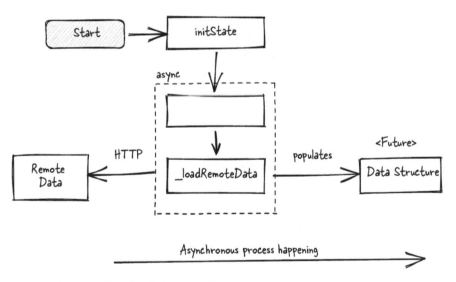

Figure 13-6. Remote data loading example

The *dart:async* package is used to perform an asynchronous operation for network calls. Additionally, the *dart:convert* package is required, as the API to be used returns JSON. Ensure these packages have been added to your application before attempting to use them (see Recipe 8.5 for adding packages to Flutter).

Using the *HTTP* package in Dart significantly simplifies the process of retrieving external data. Similar to the examples for local and embedded data, the remote option declares a `_loadRemoteData` option. In this method we make a remote call to the Uniform Resource Identifier (URI) containing our file to be downloaded. The call will return a response that includes a status code that needs to be checked to ascertain whether we have been successful or not with our request.

When working with remote data, be mindful of the response codes returned. In general, HTTP 200 represents a successful response, HTTP 400 indicates an error in the request, and 500 indicates a server error. Having a remote endpoint that conforms with generally accepted HTTP return codes can save a lot of debugging effort.

If the response is valid (i.e., HTTP 200), we can return the response body that contains the JSON data requested. The request uses a `Future` to tell our application that we are using asynchronous calls. Use a `Future` when loading external data, especially when you don't know how big the data to be retrieved is. Moving the remote data access to an asynchronous call will help the general performance of your application by not blocking the presentation layer.

Once the data has been downloaded, you can process it in the normal manner, depending on your application needs.

## CHAPTER 14

Testing the Flutter User Interface

In this chapter, you will learn how to create user interface (UI) test cases for your Flutter-based code. Creating a test for the UI can require a lot of effort, because the application responsible for interrogating the user actions needs to be aware of the elements present on-screen.

There are a number of approaches that can be taken to add UI testing to your application. First, we discuss widget testing and automated widget testing. We then explore external tools that provide the same functionality. If you are running something like a continuous integration pipeline, having the ability to run tests outside of the Flutter environment is particularly helpful, as it requires less platform scaffolding.

You will learn how to:

- Understand automated widget testing
- Integrate automated widget testing
- Use the Flutter driver
- Work with the Firebase testing suite

By the end of the chapter, you will be familiar with the options available and be able to incorporate these techniques into your own project. It is worth noting that automated testing of a UI is an evolving area, and your mileage will vary.

14.1 Automated Widget Testing in Flutter

Problem

You want a way to perform enhanced UI testing incorporating user interaction.

Solution

Use widget testing to provide additional assurance for your application. Specifically, you are able to incorporate tests for widget elements such as FloatingActionButtons, Text, and ListViews. Adding this functionality to your application will provide additional coverage for reducing overall defects. In Figure 14-1, the boilerplate counter app is used to illustrate the methods of automated testing.

Figure 14-1. Testing a Flutter UI

To test the boilerplate application generated by Flutter as in Figure 14-1, we require some code. The following test code is used to validate the on-screen elements associated with the presented application:

```
import 'package:flutter/material.dart';
import 'package:flutter_test/flutter_test.dart';

import 'package:test_widget_app/main.dart';

void main() {
  testWidgets('Counter increments smoke test', (WidgetTester tester) async {
    // Build our app and trigger a frame.
    await tester.pumpWidget(const MyApp());

    // Verify that our counter starts at 0.
    expect(find.text('0'), findsOneWidget);
```

```
    expect(find.text('1'), findsNothing);

    // Tap the '+' icon and trigger a frame.
    await tester.tap(find.byIcon(Icons.add));
    await tester.pump();

    // Verify that our counter has incremented.
    expect(find.text('0'), findsNothing);
    expect(find.text('1'), findsOneWidget);
  });
}
```

Discussion

The example code added within the Flutter project structure uses a Flutter demo app as an example. When creating this template generated by the Flutter framework, the tests incorporated are widget tests.

Widget tests have a similar signature to unit tests. The difference is they use `test Widgets`, along with a `WidgetTester`, to perform the validation of an application. Adding widget tests provides a broader scope test over a unit test. In the example, the UI is linked to the test to provide coverage of the user actions. While this provides a wider spectrum of functionality, it also increases the amount of effort associated with building tests.

A `tester.pumpWidget` is used to inflate the screen to be tested. If you have an application with multiple screens, make note to correctly invoke this method. In most examples, this uses the `MyApp` class, which is associated with the MaterialApp:

```
    // Build our app and trigger a frame.
    await tester.pumpWidget(const MyApp());
```

If you are using another screen that is the child of this class, then you will need to amend the declaration as follows:

```
    // Build our app and trigger a frame.
    await tester.pumpWidget(MaterialApp(detail: DetailPage()));
```

Accessing on-screen information can be achieved in a number of ways. In the example code, the on-screen elements are overly populated, so using the method `find.text` will suffice. If your application has a busier screen and includes more elements, an alternative method would be required. Fortunately, the `find` method includes a number of alternatives to suit most situations. I highly recommend bookmarking the `find` method if you intend to create widget tests. Personally, I use `find.byType`, `find.byWidget`, and `find.text` the most out of all the available options.

The typical use case for widget testing is to provide a validation of on-screen and user interactivity. While widget tests can be created very quickly, do consider if the use cases provide suitable application functionality coverage. In many instances, the combination of unit and widget tests can offer the best outcome, depending on the nature of your application.

14.2 Performing Automated Widget Testing

Problem

You want a way to test whether the widget UI is performing to requirements.

Solution

Use widget testing to configure your application to feature keys within the application code. This provides the widget test a clean method to find the relevant elements.

In the example, there is a username and password field defined. The widget test uses the pumpWidget and pump methods to interact with the widget:

```
void main(){
  testLoginWidget("should allow login", (WidgetTester testWorker) async {
    // Arrange
    final testUsername = find.byKey(ValueKey("testUsername"));
    final testPassword = find.byKey(ValueKey("testPassword"));
    final testLoginBtn = find.byKey(ValueKey("testLoginBtn"));

    // Act
    await testWorker.pumpWidget(MaterialApp(home: Home()));
    await testWorker.enterText(testUsername, "username");
    await testWorker.enterText(testPassword, "password");
    await testWorker.tap(testLoginBtn);
    Await testWorker.pump();

    // Assert
    expect(find.text("Login credentials supplied"), findsOneWidget);
  });
}
```

Discussion

In the example code, we create a widget test to check the home page. The home page includes a number of on-screen elements that require user interaction. Previously, we have added unit tests to ensure that the sections of code defined meet our requirements. Introducing a widget test provides another layer of refinement for your application.

Configuring an application for widget testing requires some additional effort (e.g., mapping out the on-screen information to be tested) to organize your code to make accessing information easier. The main use case for this type of testing is a UI that requires a lot of repetitive testing.

14.3 Performing Integration Testing with Flutter Driver

Problem

You want a way to test the entire application.

Solution

Use Flutter Driver, as it provides an interface driver package that will enable automated interaction with an application. The interaction automates the normal actions that would be performed by a user of the application, e.g., entering text, selecting items, and pressing buttons.

To start an integration test, create a basic interface in Flutter:

```
import 'package:flutter/material.dart';
import 'package:flutter_driver/driver_extension.dart';

void main() {
  enableFlutterDriverExtension();
  runApp(MyApp());
}

class MyApp extends StatelessWidget {
  ...
}

class MyWidget extends StatelessWidget {
  ...
}
```

Create an integration test application:

```
final txtUsername = find.byType(Text);
final btnAddition = find.byType(FloatingActionButton);

FlutterDriver driver;

setUpAll(()) async {
  driver = await FlutterDriver.connect();
});

tearDownAll(()) async {
  if (driver != null) {
    driver.close();
  }
}

test ('Should enter username and press button', ()async {
  await driver.tap(txtUsername);
  await driver.enterText("Martha Kent")
```

```
await driver.tap(btnAddition);
await driver.waitFor(find.text("Welcome"));
});
```

Discussion

In the example code, the Flutter Driver is added to the application to provide the necessary integration test facility.

To initiate the integration test, invoke the process by doing the following at the command line:

```
flutter drive --target=test_driver/main.dart
```

When the integration test is run, it will attempt to start the application and then execute the command, similar to a user.

The integration test uses an asynchronous interface to walk through your application. If you have ever run Selenium or Puppeteer, you will be familiar with this type of testing. The main effort associated with this type of testing is determining the validity of the test. In most instances, the elements on-screen will have an associated timeout, making each interaction dependent on the asynchronous wait time.

Integration testing requires a greater amount of effort over unit and widget testing. For this reason, developers typically avoid this type of testing, preferring the other types. Given the interaction with the UI, changes to the UI can mean the integration can become brittle. For example, a change in the UI could mean a logical flow is no longer valid.

In most instances when running integration testing, you would use a test (sometimes called a staging) environment. Doing this will allow you to remove/wipe the data created. Ideally, you would want an environment where you can load/delete data with freedom.

The typical use case for integration testing is where you have many repetitive tasks. Automating this scenario can make a lot of sense. However, be mindful that it can require a lot of effort to perform the initial setup and maintain the test environment. If the thought of this does not put you off, having tests automatically run through an application can be a huge time-saver.

14.4 Testing Android/iOS Device Compatibility

Problem

You want to ensure device compatibility through the use of automated testing.

Solution

Use the Firebase Test Lab's Robo tests to provide a hands-off approach to testing. The Firebase option doesn't require any additional setup and takes the application binary as an input.

Discussion

Firebase Test Lab provides a rich set of test tools for your application.

Note that at the time of writing, the Firebase test suite is specifically targeting Android and iOS. Therefore, you may wish to consider other options if you are aiming for other platforms, e.g., web, Windows, or Linux.

If you have a requirement to improve the mobile device compatibility, the Firebase Test Lab is likely the optimal solution for you and your team. Similar to other Firebase products, the billing approach is based on Spark (limited tests on 5 physical/10 virtual devices) and Blaze (billed by the minute).

Firebase Test Lab is based on multiple products. Each product is aimed at delivering against the key phases of the quality assurance lifecycle. Using the Test Lab means applications can be tested without additional coding effort by loading the Flutter application binary file. Firebase Test Lab can integrate with an existing workflow for Android build processes to orchestrate application development. The resultant tests can be performed on either physical or virtual devices to provide real-world feedback.

The application suite takes the application with debug code as an input. In the instance of Android, the Android Package Kit (APK)/Android App Bundle (AAB) will need to be provided to initiate the process. The Android binary will be found in the *build* directory. In addition, the virtual devices that the application will be deployed to will also need to be selected from a very wide selection of devices.

Lab testing can be performed in a number of ways using this test suite. Robo tests (i.e., automated testing) will run the application on a wide variety of Android devices. During these test runs, the output will be captured, specifically in terms of application crashes or notifications of defects. Additionally, there are smaller tests that incorporate instrumented tests (developer written) to access an application meeting requirements.

Robo tests on Android can be used to automatically navigate an app and perform log capture suitable for in-depth troubleshooting. Robo tests provide a lot of information for each test run, such as screenshots and video for the tests performed. If you are targeting iOS devices, XCTest performs unit, performance, and UI tests for Xcode-based projects.

The typical use case for using Firebase Test Lab is to establish the root cause of defects associated with an application. It is a very extensive solution for on-device testing, so it is highly recommended to make use of these tests even on a limited basis.

## CHAPTER 15

Working with Firebase and Flutter

In this chapter, you will learn the basics of using Firebase with Flutter. Firebase provides a suite of tools and services to simplify the building of complex applications. Central to using Firebase are the most common options of authentication and databases.

In contrast to Flutter, Firebase can be pretty intimidating, especially if you are used to working only with the frontend. While this chapter covers the most common use case for Firebase integration, it is well worth exploring the full suite to get a feel for the environment. Firebase and Flutter are perfect partners, even more so as of Google I/O 2022, as Firebase now supports Flutter as a first-party platform.

Over the course of this chapter, you will be introduced to the various billing models, setting up the backend and client environments. You will learn how to:

- Use the Firebase billing tier
- Set up a local development environment
- Work with the Firebase Emulator Suite
- Configure a Firestore database
- Write to a Firestore database
- Read from a Firestore database
- Enable Firebase Authentication

The objective of this chapter is to allow you to take advantage of the Firebase platform in your applications.

15.1 Using the Firebase Platform with Flutter

Problem

You want to understand the Firebase solution and how components relate to Flutter development.

Solution

Consult the Firebase documentation (*https://firebase.google.com*) to understand the options available. The Firebase solution provides a complete backend platform for Flutter development, including products for database, authentication, storage, and testing.

Discussion

Firebase natively supports iOS, Android, web, Unity, and Flutter at the time of writing. Adding a Firebase backend to a Flutter project requires platform setup.

Ensure you understand the available billing plans (see Recipe 15.2) before initiating a project.

The integration between Firebase and Flutter is much improved from previous revisions. In Figure 15-1, the Firebase project running on Google Cloud is connected to the local development environment. Ensure the backend project has been created via the Firebase console (*https://oreil.ly/KUQ5I*) (see Recipe 15.2) and the Flutter application is configured to work with Firebase (see Recipe 15.5) before you attempt to access the services.

The Firebase dashboard includes a range of options to assist with your development workflow. Various build services such as authentication, database, and storage are available without requiring complex development.

Adding Firebase to a Flutter application requires a series of steps on your local development machine. The assumption is that your development host has the necessary packages installed. If you have not performed this step, consult Recipe 15.3.

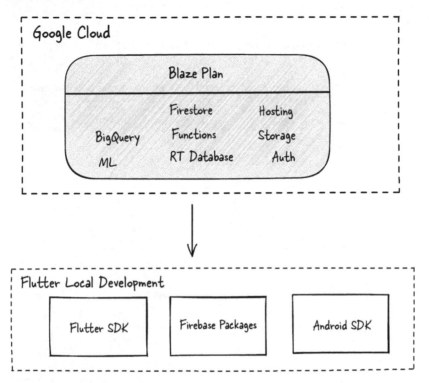

Figure 15-1. Firebase services

15.2 Setting Up a Firebase Project

Problem

You want to integrate Firebase with your Flutter application and need to set up a Firebase project.

Solution

Use the Firebase developer console (*https://oreil.ly/KUQ5I*). From here you can view all the details regarding the available services. If this is your first time visiting the console, Firebase will ask you what type of project you wish to set up.

Discussion

The creation of a new Firebase project requires you to indicate a billing plan by selecting either Spark (free tier) or Blaze (billing tier), which are shown in Figure 15-2.

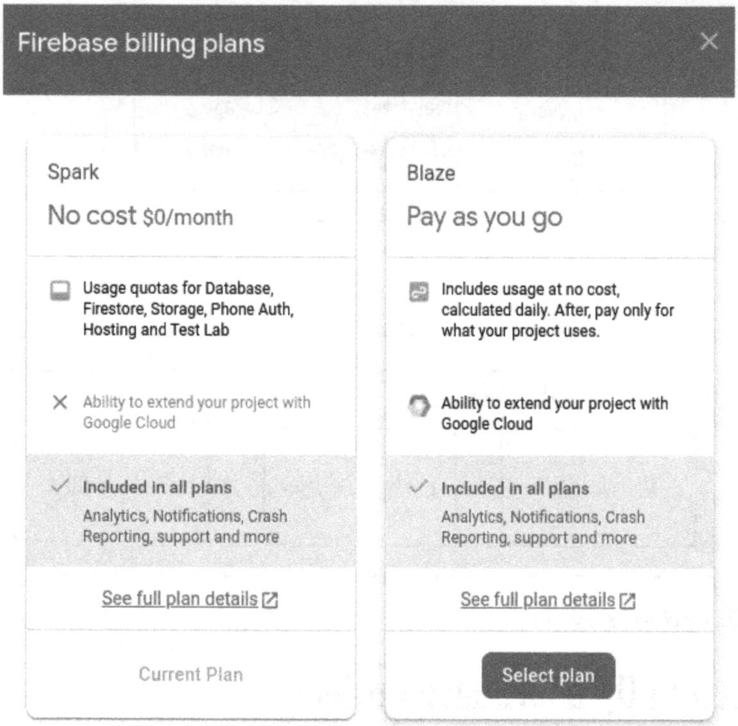

Figure 15-2. Firebase billing plans

The Spark pricing tier is typically used when starting out on development with Firebase. Spark is a no-cost (i.e., free) tier that includes limited use of the various products. Use this tier to become familiar with the various offerings from the Firebase team.

Alternatively, select the Blaze plan to access a paid tier in which to create your application. When you use a Blaze plan, it is aligned with a Google Cloud Billing account. Google Cloud Billing accounts require verified payment methods to switch to a paid account. The validity of the payment method is determined by country of origin.[1] If you choose to *delete* the Firebase project under a Blaze plan, it will also remove the

---

1 When creating a billing account, use a separate account to register for a business organization. Only use a personal account for billing when the account is for personal use.

associated Google Cloud project (including its contents). However, you can still move between the free and the paid tiers at any time.

If you are not sure which tier to use, there is also a demo project available that will enable you to test out general Firebase functionality. The demo project is a good place to start if you are unfamiliar with Firebase. From here you can view the various products and features before committing to an actual payment plan.

When creating a project, you will always be asked to accept the terms and conditions associated with using Firebase. In addition, you will need to confirm the billing plan to be used for your project and also whether you wish to include Google Analytics. The inclusion of Google Analytics is optional; it is typically used if you wish to track advertising on your application.

Firebase continues to offer a wide range of products and features that make development more approachable. The most commonly used products are Firebase Authentication, Cloud Firestore, and Firebase Hosting. Each of these products will save you a tremendous amount of development time, but they do have a learning curve associated with them.

15.3 Initializing the Firebase SDK for Local Development

Problem

You want to use Firebase local development tooling on a local machine to work with Flutter.

Solution

Use the Firebase software development kit (*https://oreil.ly/d1oYg*) (SDK) to provide a local machine with the ability to interact with the Firebase product suite. To use the SDK, you will need to have a suitable version of Node.js (*https://nodejs.org*) available on your machine.

Here's an example of how to load the Firebase SDK onto a local machine that already has Node.js installed:

```
npm install  --location=global firebase firebase-tools
```

 If you want to use the Firebase emulators, you also need to install the Java SDK in your development environment.

Discussion

By installing the Firebase SDK, you gain access to a suite of tools used to manage the Firebase environment. The SDK installation process is dependent on Node.js, so ensure you have validated compatibility with the latest version of the Firebase SDK. Figure 15-3 illustrates the software stack available on the target device once installation is complete.

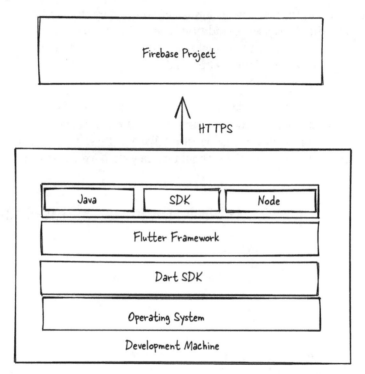

Figure 15-3. Firebase local development

Installation of the Firebase SDK is optional, as most of the products can be configured via the Firebase web console. In order to communicate with the backend Firebase services, developers should prepare their environment by installing the required packages. If you already have a development environment configured, adding the SDK can be a useful addition, as it enables developers to access resources directly from their local machine.

If your machine doesn't already have Node.js installed, refer to the Node.js site (*https://nodejs.org*) for detailed instructions on adding to your development environment. Firebase requires a number of Node.js packages to be added to your environment. The minimum Node.js package manager (npm) packages to install are *firebase* and *firebase-tools*. For this installation we use the global setting, so the tools can be called from anywhere on your machine:

```
npm install  --location=global firebase firebase-tools
```

With Firebase packages installed locally on your development host, you will be able to log in with the following command:

```
firebase login [--no-localhost]
```

Use the `firebase login` command to authenticate with your Firebase project back-end. Connecting to the backend is required if you wish to manage your Firebase project from a local machine. It is also worth noting that there is an optional `no-localhost` parameter used when working with remote development environments (or secure servers that don't allow external ports).

The command will respond with a URL that needs to be pasted into your browser. At this point, you will need to answer some security questions to ensure your ID matches between the CLI and project. On successful authentication, Firebase will respond with an authorization code that should be pasted back into the command line to complete the login process.

If you need to use `firebase login` with a continuous integration/continuous delivery (CI/CD) workflow, then an alternative option is to use `firebase login:ci`. Using this option will authenticate with your Google account and provide a token on successful login. In this scenario, a token is returned, and this can be used to initiate commands with the Firebase environment as part of the CI/CD process.

If you intend to use Firebase products, you will most likely want to also add the *flutterfire_cli* utility to your system (see Recipe 15.5). Once `flutterfire` is installed, you may need to add the *.pub-cache/bin* directory to your PATH setting. Now you are able to easily integrate a remote Firebase backend project with a local Flutter development environment.

15.4 Configuring Firebase Emulators

Problem

You want to update your development environment to perform testing of Firebase products.

Solution

Use the Firebase emulators to perform localized testing in your development environment. Firebase comes with a range of tools to make local development very similar to working with the cloud-based product.

Here's an example of how to initialize a local project with the Firebase emulators:

1. Start the process from the folder where you want Firebase products to be configured (e.g., your Flutter application directory). Initialize your development environment to use Firebase:

    ```
    firebase init
    ```

2. Select the Emulators option from the Firebase features list.

3. You will need to specify the Firebase project to use for this task.

4. Select which emulators to use.

5. Confirm the port to be used per emulator.

6. Confirm if the Emulator UI is required.

7. Confirm the download of emulators.

    ```
    firebase emulators:start
    ```

 Certain products (e.g., storage, functions, or hosting) require additional configuration. Use `firebase init [product name]` to add the product specific information.

Discussion

In the example, the Firebase emulators are configured to be used as a local development environment. As part of the initialization process, select which emulators you want to download to your client environment. Each of the emulators has a default port assigned to it; *do not change these unless necessary*. Firebase emulation includes a user interface that is a good place to start when working with the emulator components.

Ensure you are already authenticated to a Firebase project and your environment has both Node.js and Java installed.

Firebase includes a number of emulators that enable you to use a local version of tooling. These tools provide the ability to work locally from your development environment without exchanging information over the internet.

To log into a Firebase project, ensure your development environment is configured with the Firebase packages (see Recipe 15.3). Logging into the Emulator Suite will provide an overview of the product and reveal whether the emulators are active, as shown in Figure 15-4.

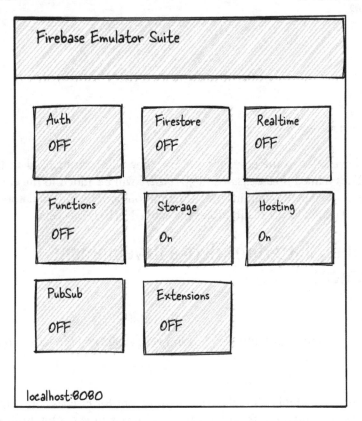

Figure 15-4. Firebase emulator

When running the Firebase Emulator Suite locally, you are presented with a view of the available components. The emulator components are a really helpful way to learn how to utilize the various Firebase tools in a local client environment. You can select which emulators are used in your project; however, bear in mind that the tools will be allocated a port on your machine. Therefore, be mindful of potential clashes if you are running other software that requires a specific port allocation.

The default emulator ports are shown in the following table, but numbers assigned are configurable if you need to allocate an alternative port:

Emulator	Port
Auth	9099
Functions	5001
Firestore	8080
Database	9000
Hosting	5000
Pub/Sub	8085
Storage	9199
UI	4000 (if available)

Once you have selected the emulators to use, they will be initialized in the current directory. Files named *firebase.json* and *.firebaserc* will be added to the current directory. The *firebase.json* file contains the configuration used by the emulators, including ports in use. The *.firebaserc* file indicates the active Firebase project.

15.5 Adding flutterfire_cli to a Development Environment

Problem

You want to integrate your Flutter application with a backend Firebase project.

Solution

Use the *flutterfire_cli* tool to initialize the environment for Firebase development. The command can be initialized from the command line and is configured for the local project.

Here's an example of how to use the *flutterfire_cli* package:

```
dart pub global activate flutterfire_cli
```

Now change to the *root* folder of your Flutter project directory, and run the following command:

```
flutterfire configure --project=[PROJECT_ID]
```

Your Flutter project is now registered with the Firebase backend project.

Discussion

In the example, the local development environment is updated to link with the back-end Firebase project.

To link the backend Firebase project with the local development Flutter application, use the `flutterfire` utility. To get started, activate the `flutterfire` command-line tool as a global reference. When you run this command, a *lib/firebase_options.dart* configuration will be added to the general profile of your machine to allow `flutter fire` to be used from anywhere.

The flutterfire command will update your configuration support (e.g., Android, iOS, web) based on the selection. On completion of the command, a new file will be generated , *lib/firebase_options.dart*, which includes the Firebase settings for the configurations set. The following is an example configuration:

```
class DefaultFirebaseOptions {
  static FirebaseOptions get currentPlatform {
    if (kIsWeb) {
      return web;
    }
    switch (defaultTargetPlatform) {
      case TargetPlatform.android:
        return android;
      case TargetPlatform.iOS:
        return ios;
      case TargetPlatform.macOS:
        throw UnsupportedError(
          'DefaultFirebaseOptions have not been configured for macos - '
          'you can reconfigure this by running the FlutterFire CLI again.',
        );
      case TargetPlatform.windows:
        throw UnsupportedError(
          'DefaultFirebaseOptions have not been configured for windows - '
          'you can reconfigure this by running the FlutterFire CLI again.',
        );
      case TargetPlatform.linux:
        throw UnsupportedError(
          'DefaultFirebaseOptions have not been configured for linux - '
          'you can reconfigure this by running the FlutterFire CLI again.',
        );
      default:
        throw UnsupportedError(
          'DefaultFirebaseOptions are not supported for this platform.',
        );
    }
  }

  static const FirebaseOptions web = FirebaseOptions(
    apiKey: 'XXXXXXXXXXXXXXX',
    appId: '9:99999999999:web:99999999999',
```

```
        messagingSenderId: '99999999999',
        projectId: 'test-firebase-999999',
        authDomain: 'test-firebase-999999.firebaseapp.com',
        storageBucket: 'test-firebase-99999.appspot.com',
    );
}
```

The file is essentially a class with definitions stating how the application should interact with a Firebase backend. Now when you wish to connect to a Firebase project, you will be able to call `flutterfire` and give it a Firebase project reference.

In your Flutter application, you will need to import the *firebase_core* package to allow the application to interact with Firebase APIs. Also, add the Firebase `initializeApp` method (*https://oreil.ly/3cPCl*) early on in your Flutter application.

15.6 Integrating a Firestore Database

Problem

You want a way to create a database as a storage solution for your Flutter application.

Solution

Use the Firestore database to persist data within your Flutter application. If you do not already have a valid Firebase project workspace, see Recipe 15.2.

Here's an example of how to set up a Firestore database within your Firebase project:

1. From the Firebase console (*https://oreil.ly/KUQ5I*), select Cloud Firestore and the create database option.
2. You will need to select either production or test mode for security rules.
3. If you are in the development phase, test mode is the quicker option to get you up and running.
4. If you set production mode, you will be required to give users access to the database, as the security rules are more strict in this mode.
5. Cloud Firestore requires a location in which it will be hosted. Location is an important consideration and enables developers to geofence data in a particular region.

Discussion

In the example, you set up a Cloud Firestore, as shown in Figure 15-5, which is a NoSQL (*https://oreil.ly/qgNPR*) database hosted in the cloud.

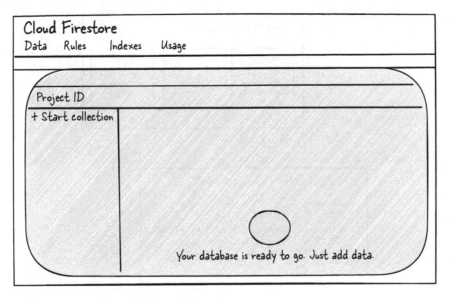

Figure 15-5. Cloud Firestore database

The use of NoSQL in Firestore is important, as this removes the data restrictions associated with the content of the database. Contrast this with a SQL database, where consistency in the model is required. NoSQL databases can include inconsistent elements within the database, making it easier to extend for different purposes without necessarily requiring a remodel.

Firestore databases must specify a location. The location cannot be changed at a later date, so ensure you select the correct region on creation. Once the location is selected, this will also act as the default for any associated Cloud Storage used.

To initialize the database, use the Firebase backend dashboard to access the user interface for the Firestore. From the Firebase dashboard, select "Firestore create database." The database provides two security settings options, i.e., *production mode* and *test mode*. In production mode, the security rules governing the database are locked down and permit read/write operations only. In contrast, test mode creates an open database with a default of 30 days of access based on time of creation. After 30 days, the rules lock down the database by default, meaning you need to either update the security rules or delete the database.

A collection is the topmost entity defined at the Firestore root. Collections are the high-level containers that provide a way to hold the database documents. In Figure 15-6, we have a collection defined for the league, which includes documents for each group of teams. Here the league represents a grouping of English football leagues. The subcollection is used to hold the specifics relating to the teams within each league.

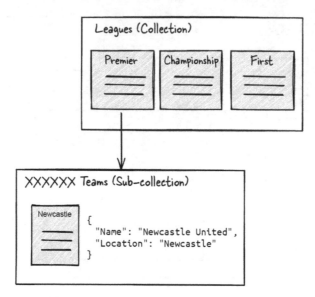

Figure 15-6. Firestore collection

A collection that has a parent is called a subcollection. Here a collection is referenced via a collection with a document pointing to another collection. The teams subcollection holds document information relating to the details per team. Within the collection, key/value pairs are used to hold data relating to the collection. In the example, there is a collection of football leagues featuring the premier league. Within this collection, we have documents defined for each football team within the premier league. The document for a football team contains details based on the team, e.g., the name and location.

Documents use fields (e.g., key/value pairs) containing the information held in the database. A document structure will be familiar to you if you have used either JavaScript objects or Python dictionaries. Documents hold the basic primitives such as strings and integers as well as Maps.

If you are developing a solution that requires the data to be hosted in a particular country, this is the setting to be sure to pay attention to. Once this setting is confirmed, the database cannot be updated to use an alternative location. With security rules and location selected, your empty database will now be available on the Firebase remote dashboard. The Cloud Firestore database can now be linked to your client project via the Firebase initialization process.

Using a NoSQL database in your application can require more defensive programming to ensure the expected data matches that which is presented. In a Flutter application, these integrity checks are performed at the client side. Thankfully, checking integrity is more important when performing database write operations. So for most applications this action should not incur too much overhead, as reads are generally the more frequent operation.

15.7 Writing Data to a Firestore Database

Problem

You want your Flutter application to write data to a Firestore database using the Firebase SDK.

Solution

Use the Firebase SDK to update a Flutter application with the ability to write to a Firestore database. To get started, update your application to include the Firebase packages with access to the backend database. If you do not already have a valid Cloud Firestore database, see Recipe 15.6. If you need to read from a Firestore database, see Recipe 15.8.

Here's an example showing how to use a Flutter application to write to a Firestore database. In the example, a basic Flutter app is used to write information directly to a database (e.g., emulator or remote):

```
import 'package:cloud_firestore/cloud_firestore.dart';
import 'package:firebase_core/firebase_core.dart';
import 'package:flutter/foundation.dart';
import 'package:flutter/material.dart';

import 'firebase_options.dart';

void main() async {
  await Firebase.initializeApp(
    options: DefaultFirebaseOptions.currentPlatform,
  );

  if (kDebugMode) {
    try {
      FirebaseFirestore.instance.useFirestoreEmulator('localhost', 8080);
    } catch (e) {
      // ignore: avoid_print
      print(e);
    }
  }

  runApp(const MyApp());
}

class MyApp extends StatelessWidget {
  const MyApp({Key? key}) : super(key: key);
```

```
      // This widget is the root of your application.
      @override
      Widget build(BuildContext context) {
        return MaterialApp(
          title: 'Firebase Firestore Demo',
          theme: ThemeData(
            primarySwatch: Colors.blue,
          ),
          home: const MyHomePage(title: 'Flutter Firestore Database: Write'),
        );
      }
    }

    class MyHomePage extends StatefulWidget {
      const MyHomePage({Key? key, required this.title}) : super(key: key);
      final String title;

      @override
      State<MyHomePage> createState() => _MyHomePageState();
    }

    class _MyHomePageState extends State<MyHomePage> {
      final _nameController = TextEditingController();
      final _locationController = TextEditingController();

      @override
      Widget build(BuildContext context) => Scaffold(
        appBar: AppBar(
          // Here we take the value from the MyHomePage object that was created by
          // the App.build method, and use it to set our AppBar title.
          title: Text(widget.title),
        ),
        body: ListView(
          padding: const EdgeInsets.all(20),
          // Center is a layout widget. It takes a single child and positions it
          // in the middle of the parent.
          children: <Widget>[
            TextField(
              decoration: const InputDecoration(
                labelText: 'Team Name',
                border: OutlineInputBorder(),
              ),
              controller: _nameController,
            ),
            const SizedBox(height: 20.0),
            TextField(
                decoration: const InputDecoration(
                  labelText: 'Team Location',
                  border: OutlineInputBorder(),
                ),
                controller: _locationController),
            const SizedBox(height: 20.0),
```

```
      ElevatedButton(
          onPressed: () {
            createTeam(
                name: _nameController.text.trim(),
                location: _locationController.text.trim());
          },
          child: const Text('Add'))
    ],
  ),
);

Future createTeam({required String name, required String location}) async {
  // Write to the Cloud Firestore database
  final docTeam = FirebaseFirestore.instance.collection('teams').doc();

  final teamJSON = {
    'name': name,
    'location': location,
  };

  // Create the document and write data
  await docTeam.set(teamJSON);

  // Add: import 'package:flutter/foundation.dart';
  // Production Debug statement
  if (kDebugMode) {
    print("Database Write!");
  }
}
}
```

On completion of the activity, confirm the data entered has been successfully written to the backend Firestore database.

Discussion

In the example code, the user is presented with a form that allows them to enter a name and location (see Figure 15-7), which will be written to the Cloud Firestore database associated with the project.

Figure 15-7. Firestore database write example

To begin using a Firestore database, update the Flutter development environment to add the *Firebase* and *Firestore* packages. Add the packages to the environment to allow Flutter to communicate with Firebase.

```
flutter pub add firebase_core
flutter pub add cloud_firestore
```

If you have already linked your project with a Firebase backend using *flutterfire_cli* (see Recipe 15.5), your application can now interact with the backend. Writing information to a Cloud Firestore database requires a valid reference to the backend project and associated database.

Running the application will enable the user to enter their favorite team and click the Add button. At this point the information entered on-screen will be written to the Firestore database linked with the project, as illustrated in Figure 15-8.

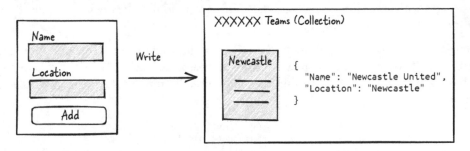

Figure 15-8. Write data to a Firestore database

 The following lines will attempt to use the Firebase Firestore emulator if available; otherwise, the application will look to use the remote backend:

```
if (kDebugMode) {
  try {
    FirebaseFirestore.instance.useFirestoreEmulator
      ('localhost', 8080);
    await FirebaseAuth.instance.useAuthEmulator
      ('localhost', 9099);
  } catch (e) {
    // ignore: avoid_print
    print(e);
  }
}
```

The database collection name (i.e., teams) is used to identify the correct database in which to persist information. The Firebase Cloud Firestore expects data to be presented in JavaScript Object Notation (JSON) format and written to the database document as a key/value pair. If you are unfamiliar with handling JSON data, you can refer to Recipe 13.5.

15.8 Reading Data from Cloud Firestore

Problem

You want your Flutter application to read data from an existing Cloud Firestore database using the Firebase SDK.

Solution

Use the Firebase SDK to update a Flutter application with the ability to read a Firestore database. To get started, update your application to include the Firebase packages with access to the backend database. If you do not already have a valid Firestore database, see Recipe 15.6.

Here's an example showing how to use a Flutter application to read from a Firestore database. If you need to write to a Firestore database, see Recipe 15.7. In the example, a basic Flutter app is used to read information directly from a database (e.g., emulator or remote):

```
import 'package:cloud_firestore/cloud_firestore.dart';
import 'package:firebase_core/firebase_core.dart';
import 'package:flutter/foundation.dart';
import 'package:flutter/material.dart';

import 'firebase_options.dart';

void main() async {
  await Firebase.initializeApp(
    options: DefaultFirebaseOptions.currentPlatform,
  );

  if (kDebugMode) {
   try {
     FirebaseFirestore.instance.useFirestoreEmulator('localhost', 8080);
   } catch (e) {
     // ignore: avoid_print
     print(e);
   }
  }

  runApp(const MyApp());
}

class MyApp extends StatelessWidget {
  const MyApp({Key? key}) : super(key: key);

  // This widget is the root of your application.
  @override
  Widget build(BuildContext context) {
    return MaterialApp(
      title: 'Firestore Demo',
      theme: ThemeData(
        primarySwatch: Colors.blue,
      ),
      home: const MyHomePage(title: 'Flutter Firestore Database: Read'),
    );
  }
}

class MyHomePage extends StatefulWidget {
  const MyHomePage({Key? key, required this.title}) : super(key: key);
  final String title;
```

```dart
  @override
  State<MyHomePage> createState() => _MyHomePageState();
}

class _MyHomePageState extends State<MyHomePage> {

  @override
  Widget build(BuildContext context) => Scaffold(
    appBar: AppBar(
      // Here we take the value from the MyHomePage object that was created by
      // the App.build method, and use it to set our AppBar title.
      title: Text(widget.title),
    ),
    body: StreamBuilder<List<Team>>(
      builder: (context, snapshot) {
        if (snapshot.hasError) {
          return const Text('Unable to read Cloud Firestore');
        } else if (snapshot.hasData) {
          final dbteams = snapshot.data!;

          return ListView(children: dbteams.map(buildTeam).toList());
        } else {
          return const Center(
            child: CircularProgressIndicator(),
          );
        }
      },
      stream: readTeams(),
    ),
  );

  Widget buildTeam(Team team) => ListTile(
    leading: const CircleAvatar(child: Text('Prem')),
    title: Text(team.name),
    subtitle: Text(team.location),
  );

  Future createTeam({required String name, required String location}) async {
    // Write to the Cloud Firestore database
    final docTeam = FirebaseFirestore.instance.collection('Teams').doc();

    final teamJSON = {
      'name': name,
      'location': location,
    };

    // Create the document and write data
    await docTeam.set(teamJSON);

    // Add: import 'package:flutter/foundation.dart';
    // Production Debug statement
    if (kDebugMode) {
```

```
      print("Database Write!");
    }
  }

  Stream<List<Team>> readTeams() => FirebaseFirestore.instance
      .collection('teams')
      .snapshots()
      .map((snapshot) =>
      snapshot.docs.map((doc) => Team.fromJson(doc.data())).toList());
}

class Team {
  // String id;
  final String name;
  final String location;

  Team({
    // this.id = '',
    required this.name,
    required this.location,
  });

  Map<String, dynamic> toJson() => {
    // 'id': id,
    'name': name,
    'location': location,
  };

  static Team fromJson(Map<String, dynamic> json) => Team(
    // id: json['id'],
      name: json['name'],
      location: json['location']);
}
```

Discussion

In the example code, the user is presented a data read from a Cloud Firestore database containing information about football teams, as shown in Figure 15-9.

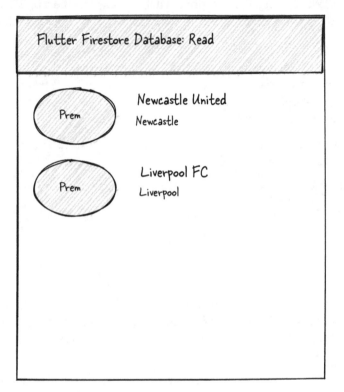

Figure 15-9. Firestore database read example

The code will display any information found in the database and reads from the defined collection (i.e., teams). For each data item found, the information will be added to a ListView to be displayed to the user, as shown in Figure 15-10.

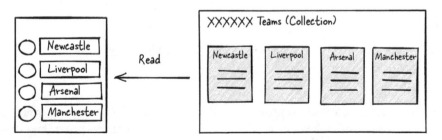

Figure 15-10. Read data from a Firestore database

The database collection is labeled "teams" and can be updated independently of the Flutter application.

Ensure you have linked your project with a Firebase backend using *flutterfire_cli* (see Recipe 15.5). When using the Firestore database, ensure the application has also added the Firebase packages to access the backend Firebase project, as shown:

```
flutter pub add firebase_core cloud_firestore
```

When you read information from a Cloud Firestore database, you use the collection identifier to reference the correct data. Information is streamed from the database to the Flutter application. Any changes made to the backend database will be immediately accessible on the frontend.

The following lines will attempt to use the Firebase Firestore emulator if available; otherwise, the application will look to use the remote backend:

```
if (kDebugMode) {
  try {
    FirebaseFirestore.instance.useFirestoreEmulator('localhost', 8080);
  } catch (e) {
    // ignore: avoid_print
    print(e);
  }
}
```

Data that you read from the database is supplied to the Flutter application as JSON. If you are unfamiliar with handling JSON data, you can refer to Recipe 13.5. Once the data is loaded from the database, the information can be presented on-screen using the normal widget creation process.

When handing the data, the example uses a StreamBuilder to validate the state of the data returned. If an error occurs, then a message is presented to the user to indicate the database could not be read. Otherwise, the data is valid and can be presented to the user.

15.9 Adding Firebase Authentication to Flutter

Problem

You want to include the use of authentication in your Flutter application.

Solution

Use Firebase Authentication to provide a wide range of credential types in your application. Firebase enables developers to select a number of different provider authentication solutions.

Here's an example of how to integrate email-based authentication into a Flutter application to access an existing user:

```dart
import 'dart:html';

import 'package:flutter/material.dart';
import 'package:flutter/foundation.dart';
import 'package:firebase_auth/firebase_auth.dart';
import 'package:firebase_core/firebase_core.dart';
import 'firebase_options.dart';

void main() async {
  await Firebase.initializeApp(
    options: DefaultFirebaseOptions.currentPlatform,
  );

  if (kDebugMode) {
    try {
      await FirebaseAuth.instance.useAuthEmulator('localhost', 9099);
    } catch (e) {
      // ignore: avoid_print
      print(e);
    }
  }

  runApp(const MyApp());
}

class MyApp extends StatelessWidget {
  const MyApp({Key? key}) : super(key: key);

  @override
  Widget build(BuildContext context) {
    return const MaterialApp(
      debugShowCheckedModeBanner: false,
      home: MainPage(),
    );
  }
}

class MainPage extends StatelessWidget {
  const MainPage({Key? key}) : super(key: key);

  @override
  Widget build(BuildContext context) {
    return Scaffold(
        body: StreamBuilder<User?>(
            stream: FirebaseAuth.instance.authStateChanges(),
            builder: (context, snapshot) {
              if (snapshot.hasData) {
                return const HomePage();
              } else {
```

```dart
          return const LoginPage();
        }
      }));
  }
}

class HomePage extends StatelessWidget {
  const HomePage({Key? key}) : super(key: key);

  // Perform Email/Password Login
  Future signOut() async {
    await FirebaseAuth.instance.signOut();
  }

  @override
  Widget build(BuildContext context) {
    return Scaffold(
      body: Column(
        children: [
          Text('User + ${FirebaseAuth.instance.currentUser?.email}'),
          const SizedBox(height: 10.0),
          Padding(
              padding: const EdgeInsets.symmetric(horizontal: 25.0),
              child: GestureDetector(
                onTap: signOut,
                child: Container(
                  padding: const EdgeInsets.all(20),
                  decoration: BoxDecoration(
                    color: Colors.blue,
                    borderRadius: BorderRadius.circular(12),
                  ),
                  child: const Center(
                    child: Text('Sign Out'),
                  ),
                ),
              ))
        ],
      ),
    );
  }
}

class LoginPage extends StatefulWidget {
  const LoginPage({Key? key}) : super(key: key);

  @override
  State<LoginPage> createState() => _LoginPageState();
}

class _LoginPageState extends State<LoginPage> {
  // Add Controllers for Text Fields
  final _userEmailController = TextEditingController();
```

```dart
final _userPasswordController = TextEditingController();

// Perform Email/Password Login
Future signIn() async {
  await FirebaseAuth.instance.signInWithEmailAndPassword(
      email: _userEmailController.text.trim(),
      password: _userPasswordController.text.trim());
}

@override
void dispose() {
  _userEmailController.dispose();
  _userPasswordController.dispose();

  super.dispose();
}

@override
Widget build(BuildContext context) {
  return Scaffold(
      backgroundColor: Colors.grey[300],
      body: SafeArea(
          child: Center(
        child: SingleChildScrollView(
            child: Column(
          mainAxisAlignment: MainAxisAlignment.center,
          children: [
            const Text('Header'),
            const SizedBox(height: 10),
            Padding(
                padding: const EdgeInsets.symmetric(horizontal: 25.0),
                child: TextField(
                  controller: _userEmailController,
                  decoration: const InputDecoration(hintText: 'Email'),
                )),
            const SizedBox(
              height: 10,
            ),
            Padding(
                padding: const EdgeInsets.symmetric(horizontal: 25.0),
                child: TextField(
                  controller: _userPasswordController,
                  obscureText: true,
                  decoration: const InputDecoration(hintText: 'Password'),
                )),
            const SizedBox(
              height: 10,
            ),
            Padding(
                padding: const EdgeInsets.symmetric(horizontal: 25.0),
                child: GestureDetector(
                  onTap: signIn,
```

```
                child: Container(
                  padding: const EdgeInsets.all(20),
                  decoration: BoxDecoration(
                    color: Colors.blue,
                    borderRadius: BorderRadius.circular(12),
                  ),
                  child: const Center(
                    child: Text('Sign In'),
                  ),
                ),
              )),
          ],
        )),
      )));
    }
  }
```

The Flutter application will now include authentication based on the email provider and request credentials.

Discussion

In the example code, an email authentication provider is added to the Flutter application, as shown in Figure 15-11. Add Firebase Authentication support in your application to provide the major authentication methods, including Google, Twitter, Facebook, and GitHub.

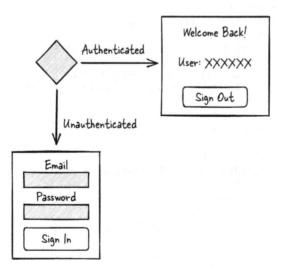

Figure 15-11. Firebase Authentication workflow

To configure your local Flutter project with a Firebase backend, use *flutterfire_cli* (see Recipe 15.5). A Firebase configuration file is used to connect the backend project with the Flutter application.

Enter an example user complete with email address and password to test the authentication via the Flutter application. The application is based on two screens that illustrate the sign-in workflow used by Firebase. In the code, a preexisting (unauthenticated) user is required to sign in. Once the user has signed in, they will be presented with a second page, where they can sign out. Flutter is used to maintain the authenticated state of the user and display the relevant page.

The following lines will attempt to use the Firebase Authentication emulator if available; otherwise, the application will look to use the remote backend. Authentication provides an additional notification to let you know you are using the emulator as a security precaution:

```
if (kDebugMode) {
  try {
    await FirebaseAuth.instance.useAuthEmulator('localhost', 9099);
  } catch (e) {
    // ignore: avoid_print
    print(e);
  }
}
```

To set up authentication at the backend, visit the Firebase dashboard (*https://oreil.ly/ KUQ5I*) to add authentication to the project. At this point you see a range of providers; in Figure 15-12, the email provider setup is shown.

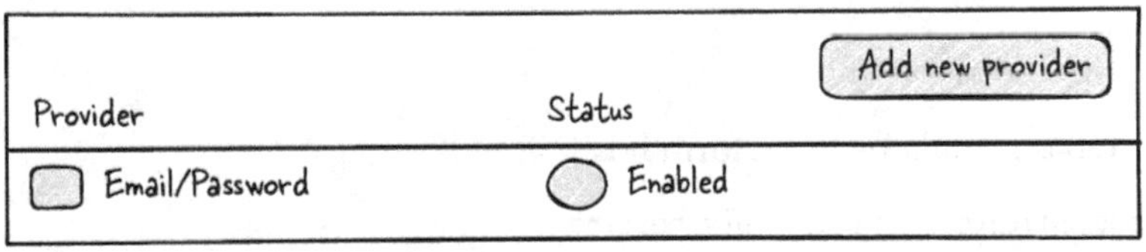

Figure 15-12. Adding a Firebase Authentication provider

If you need to use an "Additional providers" authentication, you will need to conform to the provider requirements. The required information is dependent on the provider, so be sure to read the configuration requirements when setting up the authentication. Once a provider has been configured in Firebase Authentication, it will need to be enabled in your Flutter application.

15.10 Using Flutter Web with Firebase Hosting

Problem

You want to host a Flutter web application using the Firebase Emulator Suite.

Solution

Use the Firebase Emulator Suite to host your Flutter application locally. From your Flutter build environment, create a web-based application and deploy it to Firebase Hosting.

Here's an example of how to set up Firebase Emulator Suite to perform local hosting:

1. Start from the root of the Flutter project directory, e.g., *[test_app]*:
   ```
   firebase init
   ```
2. Tell the Firebase Emulator Suite you want to use hosting.
   a. Select "Hosting: Configure files for Firebase Hosting and (optionally) set up GitHub Action deploys"
   b. What do you want to use as your public directory? **build/web**[2]
   c. Configure as a single-page app (rewrite all URLs to */index.html*)? **No**
   d. Set up automatic builds and deploys with GitHub? **No**

Build the Flutter code as a web application. The default output is to *[test_app]/build/web*:

```
flutter build web
```

Run the Firebase emulator to perform hosting:

```
firebase emulators:start --only hosting
```

The application will now be displayed in the hosting session in the browser, i.e., *localhost:5000*.

Discussion

In the example, Firebase Emulator Suite hosting, shown in Figure 15-13, is used to run a Flutter application. When running the emulator we use the `-- hosting` extension to only use the resources required. If you were to run the command without this extension, all configured emulator tools would be started.

---

2 The *build/web* folder is associated with the Flutter web configuration.

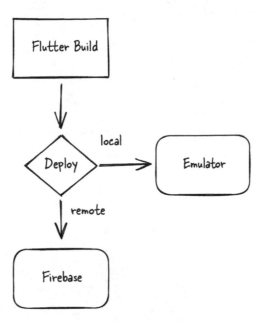

Figure 15-13. Firebase Emulator Suite hosting example

You can use this process to temporarily host a Flutter application on a local machine running the Firebase Emulator Suite. Firebase is able to intelligently determine the correct destination, as shown in Figure 15-13. The application will be available in the web browser using the address associated with the Firebase Hosting UI (e.g., *localhost:5000*).

## CHAPTER 16

Introducing Cloud Services

In this chapter, you will learn how to integrate Flutter and Dart with cloud provider services. The first question you may ask is, Why would I use cloud services? Well, as you build more advanced applications that go beyond the mobile/desktop platform, you need somewhere to run/host your code. Using cloud services enables your application to utilize a variety of extensive services such as APIs, storage, authentication, and databases. But wait, don't I get that with Firebase? Well, you do, but Firebase is but an appetizer for the main course.

Over the course of this chapter, we use Google Cloud as the basis for examples; however, the techniques apply to most cloud providers' solutions. At the point of deployment, we will be introducing technology to minimize infrastructure configuration, i.e., serverless. Serverless relates to reduction of overhead associated with infrastructure set requirements.

You will learn how to:

- Get started with identity and access management
- Use Cloud Storage as a backend
- Develop a simple HTTP server
- Migrate an application to a container
- Deploy a container to a cloud provider

Cloud services continue to evolve, which provides developers with some amazing services to access via a pay-as-you-go model. The flexibility and performance offered by cloud services will give you a good kind of development headache. The objective of this chapter is to enable you to take advantage of the Firebase platform in your applications.

16.1 Getting Started with Cloud Providers

Problem

You want a way to access a remote resource on a cloud provider such as Amazon Web Services (AWS), Microsoft Azure, or Google Cloud.

Solution

Using a cloud provider will typically include a free tier to enable you to get started. You will be required to register with the cloud service provider to get access to the available products.

Over the course of this chapter, we will use Google Cloud to demonstrate particular services. We will point out cases where there is not an appropriate alternative.

Discussion

When you begin working with a cloud service provider, it can feel a bit overwhelming. Each of the cloud providers mentioned provides lots of different solutions. The main areas we will focus on are data storage and implementing a serverless infrastructure. To achieve this, we will need to consider identity and access management, which is used to authorize the credentials used with your new resource.

16.2 Working with Identity and Access Management

Problem

You want a way to add a user account that will enable you to access cloud services.

Solution

Use the cloud to provide identity and access management settings to set constraints on user role definition and permissions. The top players in the cloud market all refer to this as identity and access management.

Discussion

Identity and access management is a fundamental concept when using any cloud provider. In general, you need to understand the two key elements, identity and access, as shown in Figure 16-1.

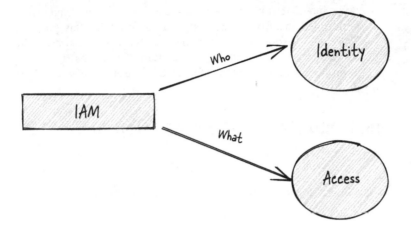

Figure 16-1. Identity and access

Cloud providers use credentials to determine the nature of permissions applicable to an account. Most providers allow the use of an email account to act as the user credential (i.e., the identity). To add a credential on your provider, enter your credentials and select a role (i.e., the access to be provided) to be associated with the credential.

Each cloud provider has its own method for adding credentials to identity and access management. The identity and access management workflow performs two tasks. First, it registers a user credential; this step tells the system who you are. Second, access management is used to determine what permissions are assigned to your user. The combination of identity and access management provides the basis for any activities performed on a cloud provider.

Identity reflects the credential that will be used to access the cloud provider, such as the email account to be associated with your cloud environment. Identity credentials are required to access the resources and authorize what can be done from there. In many ways, accessing cloud resources is similar to accessing a local machine.

Once an identity has been created, the next step is to allocate user access permissions. Access reflects the nature of permission associated with an identity. The notion of least privilege is especially important in relation to account credentials. Cloud providers will present a range of roles that are aligned with the services to be used. Applying a level of granularity provides the end user with the capability to reduce permissions down to only those necessary for the task.

Each cloud provider has its own roles/permissions used to provide access to cloud resources. Learning the difference between the access permissions will make your environment more secure. It is important not to overload a permission and follow least privilege to deliver a more secure access methodology.

If you intend to run services from a cloud provider, it is highly recommended that you create a separate account for this purpose. Sharing an account across personal and business accounts, while convenient, does not provide a separation of concerns. Therefore, always use a unique account for business-related activities where practical.

16.3 Using Cloud Storage to Host an Object

Problem

You want to use object storage as part of your Flutter application.

Solution

Cloud Storage is a great solution for sharing information over the internet. Even better, it can be accessed as an unauthenticated source (i.e., public access).

Here's an example of how to temporarily serve a file using Cloud Storage:

1. Create a Cloud Storage bucket on your cloud provider using the Cloud Console. As it will be used for data storage, best practice is to use a location as close to the requester as possible. Using a geographically dispersed bucket is helpful where you need to serve a distributed audience.

2. Make the bucket and contents public so it can be accessed without requiring authentication.

3. Add read-only access to the bucket to prevent external sources updating the data source.

4. Upload a test file to confirm the access permissions and that the storage bucket is reachable from the public internet.

5. Test access using the `curl` command:
   ```
   curl --request GET [STORAGE_ENDPOINT]/[PATH]/[FILE]
   ```

For an example of a Flutter application capable of consuming a remote JSON file, see Recipe 13.4.

Discussion

In the example, a Cloud Storage bucket is used as a backend to serve a file. Object storage provides a versatile technology that can be used for a wide number of requirements. In addition, Cloud Storage also supports an API that can be used to directly access the contents programmatically.

Understanding the product name will be beneficial to getting started with Cloud Storage. On Google Cloud, this type of storage is called Google Cloud Storage (or GCS). AWS refers to this storage as a Simple Storage Service (or S3). Azure has the name Blob Storage. Each of the offerings provides secure object storage that can be useful in a number of use cases.

Using Cloud Storage to create a hosting solution is a smart application of the technology. While you could create a small application to provide the necessary API interaction, Cloud Storage provides a very accessible no-code solution.

Content held in Cloud Storage will also have object metadata. In this context, metadata represents key/value pairs that are used by the browser when rendering the content. For our JSON file example, the Content-Type is set to *application/json*. One useful setting to be aware of is the Cache-Control setting, which determines how long the object should be cached. For example, on Google Cloud, the cache setting is located in the metadata section. To reduce caching for stored public content, add public, max-age=15 to the Cache-Control section of the object metadata page.

Be aware that cloud providers may have different defaults applied. Google Cloud has a default duration of one hour (i.e., 3,600 seconds). AWS has a default duration of 24 hours (i.e., 86,400 seconds). If you intend to make changes to the content during development, you may wish to decrease the cache duration to five minutes (i.e., 300 seconds).

Hosting information in Cloud Storage means that the information is also subject to object lifecycle management, which means you can automatically apply archive and deletion events based on a condition. Cloud Storage can be used for short-/long-term storage; however, it can also be used for static web hosting and as a file system.

16.4 Developing a Backend HTTP Server with Dart

Problem

You want to use Dart to provide a backend HTTP server.

Solution

Use the *HTTP* package to build HTTP functionality using the Dart SDK. The Dart language is capable of building backend services to support a wide range of requirements.

Here's an example of how to build a basic HTTP server that provides GET and POST routes. Create a new Dart application named *dart_test_http*:

```
import 'dart:convert';
import 'dart:io';
```

```
const port = 8080;

Future<void> main(List<String> arguments) async {
  final httpServer = await createHTTPServer();
  await httpRequest(httpServer);
}

Future<HttpServer> createHTTPServer() async {
  final intAddress = InternetAddress.anyIPv4;
  return await HttpServer.bind(intAddress, port);
}

Future<void> httpRequest(HttpServer server) async {
  await for (HttpRequest request in server) {

    if (request.method == 'GET'){
      request.response
        ..write('
            { "data": [
            {"title": "January"},
            {"title:": "February"},
            {"title": "March"}
            ] }\n')
        ..close();
    }
  }
}
```

Discussion

In the code example, Dart is used to build a simple server that will respond to HTTP verbs (*https://oreil.ly/fU_ty*) requesting information. The application is written in Dart and demonstrates how to build backend services.

Test run the application, and then use the `curl` command to send a `GET` request to the running application:

```
curl localhost:8080
```

The response from the `curl` command will return a JSON string similar to that seen in earlier chapters:

```
{ "data": [ {"title": "January"}, {"title:": "February"}, {"title": "March"} ] }
```

The Dart code is set to listen on port 8080, and when it receives a request, it will respond with the JSON payload shown in the preceding example.

From the code, you can see it is possible to use a Dart backend to serve JSON (or another format) to serve a frontend application. The application demonstrates a basic HTTP server and can be extended to cover other use cases, e.g., POST/DELETE/UPDATE.

16.5 Building a Dart Container

Problem

You want to package a Dart application to enable it to be run on a machine without access to the Dart SDK.

Solution

Use a container to package a Dart application and make it transferable to environments without access to the Dart SDK. A container is a high-level standalone executable package that includes application code and runtime libraries, making it capable of running independently of the host operating system.

Here's an example of how to package a Dart application in a container capable of running outside of the local development environment. Use the application defined in Recipe 16.4:

1. Set the working directory to the Dart example from Recipe 16.4.
2. Create a Dockerfile (see template (*https://oreil.ly/-wYbj*)):

```
FROM dart:stable AS build

# Resolve app dependencies.
WORKDIR /app
COPY pubspec.* ./
RUN dart pub get

ENV DART_FILE dart_test_http.dart

# Copy app source code and AOT compile it.
COPY . .
# Ensure packages are still up-to-date if anything has changed
RUN dart pub get --offline
#RUN dart pub run build_runner build --delete-conflicting-outputs
RUN dart compile exe bin/$DART_FILE -o bin/server

# Build minimal serving image from AOT-compiled
# `/server` and required system
# libraries and configuration files stored in `/runtime/`
# from the build stage.
FROM scratch
COPY --from=build /runtime/ /
COPY --from=build /app/bin/server /app/bin/

# Start server.
EXPOSE 8080
CMD ["/app/bin/server"]
```

3. Edit the `DART_FILE` environment variable to the name of your Dart application.

4. Build the container:
   ```
   docker build -t dart_http_server .
   ```

5. Run the container locally to test:
   ```
   docker run -d --rm -p 8080:8080 dart_http_server
   ```

6. Run a curl against the server to confirm it is working:
   ```
   curl localhost:8080
   ```

7. Quit the running container:
   ```
   docker stop $(docker ps -aq)
   ```

Discussion

In the code example, the open source Docker Engine (*https://oreil.ly/62Zs7*) utility is used to create a container image that can be run independently of the Dart SDK.

If you don't have Docker available on your machine, you can find installation instructions at Get Started with Docker (*https://oreil.ly/i0-1P*).

The build process takes account of the Dart code and copies across files for the application.

Once the build completes, you can run the container in any environment that supports the container runtime interface. The container image will reside on the machine where it was built. As per the noncontainer version, you use the `curl` command to send a request to the container running on port 8080 to receive the application payload, as shown in the following example:

```
{ "data": [ {"title": "January"}, {"title:": "February"}, {"title": "March"} ] }
```

16.6 Introducing Serverless with Dart

Problem

You want to deploy a Dart application as a container in the cloud.

Solution

Use a serverless product from a cloud provider to manage your deployment needs. Serverless relates to the ability to build and run applications without provisioning and managing backend infrastructure. Each cloud provider has its own version of this technology, so in this example, we look at Cloud Run from Google Cloud.

Here's an example of how to deploy a Dart container running Dart code to Cloud Run. The deployed application is the container outlined in Recipe 16.5:

```
gcloud run deploy dart-server --source . --region europe-west9
```

Use a `curl` command to interact with the `HTTP GET` method for the API:

```
curl --request GET [CLOUD_RUN_ENDPOINT]
```

Discussion

In the example, we take a Dart application complete with a Dockerfile manifest and deploy it to the cloud in one command. Once the command is deployed, we can run a `curl` on the application endpoint to have it return our JSON output.

While the command entered is simple, there is actually a lot going on in the background, so let's unpack it. The application directory includes the source code and a container instruction list. When we run the `gcloud` command, it is essentially asking for a workflow to upload the sources, build the container, set an identity and access management policy, and deploy the resulting container image to Cloud Run in the requested geographical region.

In this scenario, consider that you didn't add a machine specification, where to build the image, or what routing to apply or create a storage object. Instead, the cloud provider makes some assumptions about your environment and applies them to the deployment. Welcome to the serverless world. If you are not familiar with serverless, the definition can be a bit confusing. In more simple terms, it aims to remove the complexity associated with deploying general resources to the cloud.

One thing to note about serverless products is that each cloud provider has a very opinionated version of how such products should work. If you are using other cloud providers, the service equivalents to look out for are AWS Lambda and Azure Container Apps.

## CHAPTER 17

Starting with Game Development

In this chapter, you will learn how to get started developing games using Flutter. We will explain the open source Flame package, which can be used for arcade-based games. Working with it resembles working with a game engine. As you might expect, Flame is open source and features a community effort to improve the codebase.

In this chapter, the basics of Flame will be discussed with some example code. Writing games can be tremendous fun, and it also teaches you a lot about the different styles of algorithms and data structures. However, getting started can sometimes be a challenge, so the first recipe discusses adding the Flame package. Beyond that, we cover the bare essentials to provide enough knowledge to build a basic 2D game. Learning how to add basic elements to the screen, write text, control user input, and perform some basic math will enable you to write your first games.

You will learn how to:

- Add the Flame package to Flutter
- Create a boilerplate application
- Add basic graphic primitives
- Add text rendering to a game
- Add audio
- Add sprites
- Add collision detection

If you are using DartPad (*https://dartpad.dev*), you can now use this editor, as it has been updated to support Flame. I find this a good way to quickly test game code, as this provides a good compatibility layer for testing Flame boilerplate code.

Unfortunately, this chapter will not cover the Casual Games Toolkit (CGT), as at the time of writing it didn't exist. If you wish to follow the CGT path (*https://oreil.ly/Q_cwo*), I would highly recommend reading the documentation and getting involved with the discussion on the Discord server.

17.1 Adding the Flame Package to Flutter

Problem

You want a way to add the Flame package to an existing Flutter project.

Solution

Use `flutter pub add` to install the Flame package in your *pubspec.yaml*. The Flame game engine is distributed as a Flutter package.

Here's an example of how to add the Flame package to your Flutter application from the command line:

```
flutter pub add flame
```

The command will download the package and automatically update the *pubspec.yaml* file to include a reference to the latest version of the Flame game engine.

Alternatively, you can manually open the *pubspec.yaml* and add a reference to the Flame package under the dependencies section:

```
dependencies:
  flutter:
    sdk: flutter
  flame: ^1.2.0
```

Discussion

In the example, the Flame package is added to the file *pubspec.yaml*. Reference pub.dev (*https://pub.dev*) to locate information on the current package and additional documentation.

Once the Flame package is successfully installed, add the `import` statement for the Flame package to the *main.dart*. Now your application will be able to reference the package methods directly:

```
import 'package:flame/game.dart';
```

You may also want to remove the default widget test code, as this will not be relevant to the Flame code to be created.

The Flame package provides a general-purpose 2D game engine specifically for the Flutter framework, and it incorporates a number of extendable components. The engine provides developers with the ability to create feature-rich games without needing to build key game complexities such as audio or physics management.

17.2 Creating a Flame Boilerplate

Problem

You want to create a starting point for working with Flame and Flutter.

Solution

Use the Flutter application creation tool to create a sample application that provides the necessary code structure. Remove the code from both the *main.dart* and the associated tests.

Here's an example of an application that has removed the Flutter defaults and added a basic Flame codebase:

```
import 'package:flame/events.dart';
import 'package:flame/flame.dart';
import 'package:flame/game.dart';
import 'package:flutter/material.dart';

void main() async {
  WidgetsFlutterBinding.ensureInitialized();
  await Flame.device.setPortrait();
  final shapeGame = GameTemplate();

  runApp(GameWidget(game: shapeGame));
}

class GameTemplate extends
FlameGame with
  HasKeyboardHandlerComponents,
HasCollisionDetection {
  @override
  Future<void> onLoad() async {
    super.onLoad();
  }
}
```

Discussion

In the example code, a GameTemplate class is declared that is called from the Flutter main application. When the application is run, a blank screen is shown as the result.

In Figure 17-1, the game viewport is defined to show the maximum surface available on the x-axis and y-axis. Our GameTemplate class is defined and set as the game property. The definition of the GameTemplate class has HasKeyboardHandler and

HasCollisionDetection included. If you are not familiar with this type of declaration, see Recipe 5.6. These class mixins are optional components; however, for our template, it makes sense to include them, as we will almost always require them. At this point the GameTemplate class has an onLoad method to allow assets to be loaded at the start of the application.

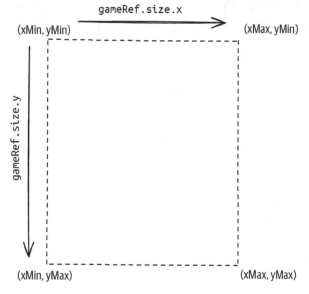

Figure 17-1. Game viewport

Flame uses a component system to provide a wide range of options for game developers. I highly recommend reading the Flame game engine page (*https://oreil.ly/w03P2*), as this has a lot of the information you will need to get started.

17.3 Adding a Sprite

Problem

You want to add an on-screen graphical image asset to the game viewport.

Solution

Use a sprite image as part of the Flame application. Loading a game asset provides a great way to improve the visuals of a game.

Here's an example showing how to add an image asset using the Flame game engine:

```
import 'package:flame/collisions.dart';
import 'package:flame/events.dart';
```

```
import 'package:flame/flame.dart';
import 'package:flame/game.dart';
import 'package:flame/components.dart';
import 'package:flutter/material.dart';

void main() async {
  WidgetsFlutterBinding.ensureInitialized();
  await Flame.device.setPortrait();
  final shapeGame = GameTemplate();
  runApp(GameWidget(game: shapeGame));
}

class GameTemplate extends FlameGame
    with HasKeyboardHandlerComponents, HasCollisionDetection {
  late Ship shipPlayer;

  @override
  Future<void> onLoad() async {
    super.onLoad();
    add(shipPlayer = Ship(await loadSprite('triangle.png')));
  }
}

class Ship extends SpriteComponent
    with HasGameRef<GameTemplate>, CollisionCallbacks {
  Ship(Sprite sprite) {
    // debugMode = true;
    this.sprite = sprite;
    size = Vector2(50.0, 50.0);
    anchor = Anchor.center;
    position = Vector2(200.0, 200.0);
    add(RectangleHitbox());
  }
}
```

Discussion

In the example code, a new class is created to represent a space ship. The class Ship
extends the SpriteComponent. Our new class therefore has access to the properties
and methods associated with the superclass. If you are not familiar with object-
oriented inheritance, see Recipe 5.4.

As shown in Figure 17-2, the sprite position is set using *x, y* coordinates and the
width and height. A Vector2 is a class that accepts two double values. As both items
take two properties, we use Vector2 to hold the relevant property information.

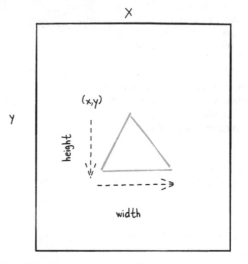

Figure 17-2. Sprite dimensions

An add method is used in the onLoad() methods to reference the Ship object. Here we pass an image available in the assets folder of the Flutter application to the Ship constructor. The Ship class takes the image and stores the value.

Take note of the z-order for items rendered on-screen. Z-order refers to the overlap order of two-dimensional objects, whereby the first item (z-order of 1) will represent the first element. Subsequent items (z-order of *N*) will overlap the existing items. Therefore, the last item to be drawn is at the top of the z-order and is not obscured by any preceding images, while the first item to be drawn will be obscured by any overlapping image.

17.4 Adding Manual Horizontal Movement to a Sprite

Problem

You want to add horizontal movement to a sprite component built using the Flame game engine.

Solution

Use the Flame game engine to add horizontal movement based on the input required. The game engine supports a variety of interfaces, such as keyboard, taps, and gestures.

Here's an example of how to integrate keyboard inputs to control an on-screen sprite:

```dart
import 'package:flame/collisions.dart';
import 'package:flame/events.dart';
import 'package:flame/flame.dart';
import 'package:flame/game.dart';
import 'package:flame/components.dart';
import 'package:flutter/material.dart';
import 'package:flutter/services.dart';

void main() async {
  WidgetsFlutterBinding.ensureInitialized();
  await Flame.device.setPortrait();
  final shapeGame = GameTemplate();
  runApp(GameWidget(game: shapeGame));
}

class GameTemplate extends FlameGame
    with HasKeyboardHandlerComponents, HasCollisionDetection {
  late Ship shipPlayer;

  @override
  Future<void> onLoad() async {
    super.onLoad();
    add(shipPlayer = Ship(await loadSprite('triangle.png')));
  }
}

class Ship extends SpriteComponent
    with HasGameRef<GameTemplate>, CollisionCallbacks {

  final movementSpeed    = 500;
  double screenPosition = 0.0;
  bool leftPressed       = false;
  bool rightPressed      = false;

  Ship(Sprite sprite) {
    // debugMode = true;
    this.sprite = sprite;
    size = Vector2(50.0, 50.0);
    anchor = Anchor.center;
    position = Vector2(200.0, 200.0);
    add(RectangleHitbox());
    add(KeyboardListenerComponent(
        // keyUp: {
        // },
        keyDown: {
          LogicalKeyboardKey.keyA: (keysPressed) { return leftPressed  = true; },
          LogicalKeyboardKey.keyD: (keysPressed) { return rightPressed = true; },
        },
      ),
    );
  }

  @override
  void update(double dt) {
    super.update(dt);

    if (leftPressed == true){
```

```
      screenPosition = position.x - movementSpeed * dt ;
      if (screenPosition > 0 + width/2){
        position.x = screenPosition;
      }
      leftPressed = false;
    }
    if (rightPressed == true){
      screenPosition = position.x + movementSpeed * dt;
      if (screenPosition < gameRef.size.x - width/2) {
        position.x = screenPosition;
      }
      rightPressed = false;
    }
  }
 }
}
```

Discussion

In the example code, the Ship class is enhanced to include keyboard interactivity. Now when the user presses the key "A," the ship will move left. When the user presses the key "D," the ship will move right. A horizontal viewport constraint is also added so the ship cannot move beyond the boundary of the screen.

In Figure 17-3, the sprite is able to move left and right by the pressing of keys. Our game view is defined as x and y coordinates available in the gameRef object. Specifically, we use the min/max size of the screen on the x-axis to constrain horizontal movement of the player in the update method. In the update method, we have access to the delta time (dt), which indicates the time taken since the last update.

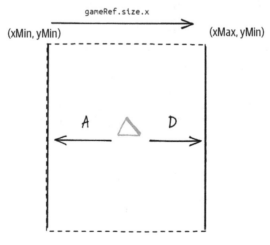

Figure 17-3. Sprite horizontal movement using the keyboard

Flame supports both Game and Component class keyboard interactivity. Keyboard events can be added directly to the Ship class using the KeyboardListenerComponent.

In this component, the `Ship` component class is given access to the keys pressed by the user. Access to the `KeyboardListenerComponent` provides you with the ability to react directly to key presses made by the user of the application. The full keyboard is available and can be set up as required. In the example code, the application responds to the two keys set up to indicate player movement.

In the situation where you require multiple components to respond to keys, it might be more practical to enable the game component (i.e., the parent) to respond to keys. Adding processing at the parent level makes propagation of key messages easier to manage. The end result is that the parent will pass a message to the relevant component (i.e., the child).

17.5 Adding Automated Vertical Movement to a Sprite

Problem

You want to add vertical movement to a sprite component built using the Flame game engine.

Solution

Use the Flame game engine to automatically apply vertical movement without user interaction. Movement is added as part of the update cycle associated with the game loop.

Here's an example of how to apply vertical movement to an on-screen sprite:

```
import 'package:flame/collisions.dart';
import 'package:flame/events.dart';
import 'package:flame/flame.dart';
import 'package:flame/game.dart';
import 'package:flame/components.dart';
import 'package:flutter/material.dart';
import 'package:flutter/services.dart';

void main() async {
  WidgetsFlutterBinding.ensureInitialized();
  await Flame.device.setPortrait();
  final shapeGame = GameTemplate();
  runApp(GameWidget(game: shapeGame));
}

class GameTemplate extends FlameGame
    with HasKeyboardHandlerComponents, HasCollisionDetection {
  late Ship shipPlayer;
  late Square squareEnemy;

  @override
```

```
    Future<void> onLoad() async {
      super.onLoad();
      add(shipPlayer = Ship(await loadSprite('triangle.png')));
      add(squareEnemy = Square(await loadSprite('square.png')));
    }
  }

  class Ship extends SpriteComponent
      with HasGameRef<GameTemplate>, CollisionCallbacks {

    final spriteVelocity  = 500;
    double screenPosition = 0.0;
    bool leftPressed       = false;
    bool rightPressed      = false;
    bool isCollision       = false;

    Ship(Sprite sprite) {
      debugMode = true;
      this.sprite = sprite;
      size = Vector2(50.0, 50.0);
      anchor = Anchor.center;
      position = Vector2(200.0, 200.0);
      add(RectangleHitbox());
      add(KeyboardListenerComponent(
          // keyUp: {
          // },
          keyDown: {
            LogicalKeyboardKey.keyA: (keysPressed) { return leftPressed  = true; },
            LogicalKeyboardKey.keyD: (keysPressed) { return rightPressed = true; },
          },
        ),
      );
    }

    @override
    void update(double dt) {
      super.update(dt);

      if (leftPressed == true){
        screenPosition = position.x - spriteVelocity * dt ;
        if (screenPosition > 0 + width/2){
          position.x = screenPosition;
        }
        print('Reset Key to false');
        leftPressed = false;
      }
      if (rightPressed == true){
        screenPosition = position.x + spriteVelocity * dt;
        if (screenPosition < gameRef.size.x - width/2) {
          position.x = screenPosition;
        }
        print('Reset Key to false');
```

```
      rightPressed = false;
    }
  }
}

class Square extends SpriteComponent
    with HasGameRef<GameTemplate>, CollisionCallbacks {

  final spriteVelocity = 100;
  double screenPosition = 0.0;

  Square(Sprite sprite) {
    debugMode = true;
    this.sprite = sprite;
    size = Vector2(50.0, 50.0);
    position = Vector2(100.0, 100.0);
    add(RectangleHitbox());
  }

  @override
  void update(double dt) {
    super.update(dt);

    // Fall down the screen
    screenPosition = position.y + spriteVelocity * dt ;
    if (screenPosition < gameRef.size.y - height/2){
        position.y = screenPosition;
    } else {
      position.y = 0;
    }
  }
}
```

Discussion

In the example code, a new Square class is used to register a sprite on-screen. The class follows the pattern outlined in Recipe 17.4, where we load an image to initialize the object.

In Figure 17-4, the sprite is set to use the y-axis to register its path down the screen. The path followed uses the y coordinate from yMin to yMax to move the sprite downward. An update method is used to amend the object position coordinates based on the y-axis of the screen viewport. For each update cycle, the object position property of y is increased, meaning it will move between the default value to a maximum of gameRef.size.y (i.e., yMax).

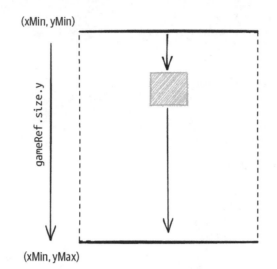

(xMin, yMin)

gameRef.size.y

(xMin, yMax)

Figure 17-4. Sprite vertical movement

To ensure the square stays within the confines of the viewport, a maximum height constraint is applied. When the object reaches the maximum height of game-Ref.size.y, the *y* position value is reset to 0.0 (i.e., reset to the top of the screen).

Based on the above, the square sprite will fall from the top of the screen on a repeating loop. The speed with which the sprite falls is controlled using the spriteVelocity variable.

17.6 Adding Collision Detection

Problem

You want to be alerted when components intersect on-screen.

Solution

Use collision detection to indicate when items are intersecting on-screen. The Flame game engine includes collision detection that can be used with components to dynamically report when this state is achieved.

Here's an example of how to add collision detection to your Flame-based application:

```
import 'package:flame/collisions.dart';
import 'package:flame/events.dart';
import 'package:flame/flame.dart';
import 'package:flame/game.dart';
import 'package:flame/components.dart';
import 'package:flutter/material.dart';
```

```dart
import 'package:flutter/services.dart';

void main() async {
  WidgetsFlutterBinding.ensureInitialized();
  await Flame.device.setPortrait();
  final shapeGame = GameTemplate();
  runApp(GameWidget(game: shapeGame));
}

class GameTemplate extends FlameGame
    with HasKeyboardHandlerComponents, HasCollisionDetection {
  late Ship shipPlayer;
  late Square squareEnemy;

  @override
  Future<void> onLoad() async {
    super.onLoad();
    add(shipPlayer = Ship(await loadSprite('triangle.png')));
    add(squareEnemy = Square(await loadSprite('square.png')));
  }
}

class Ship extends SpriteComponent
    with HasGameRef<GameTemplate>, CollisionCallbacks {

  final spriteVelocity  = 500;
  double screenPosition = 0.0;
  bool leftPressed      = false;
  bool rightPressed     = false;
  bool isCollision      = false;

  Ship(Sprite sprite) {
    debugMode = true;
    this.sprite = sprite;
    size = Vector2(50.0, 50.0);
    anchor = Anchor.center;
    position = Vector2(200.0, 200.0);
    add(RectangleHitbox());
    add(KeyboardListenerComponent(
        // keyUp: {
        // },
        keyDown: {
          LogicalKeyboardKey.keyA: (keysPressed) { return leftPressed  = true; },
          LogicalKeyboardKey.keyD: (keysPressed) { return rightPressed = true; },
        },
      ),
    );
  }

  @override
  void update(double dt) {
    super.update(dt);

    if (leftPressed == true){
      screenPosition = position.x - spriteVelocity * dt ;
      if (screenPosition > 0 + width/2){
        position.x = screenPosition;
```

```
      }
      print('Reset Key to false');
      leftPressed = false;
    }
    if (rightPressed == true){
      screenPosition = position.x + spriteVelocity * dt;
      if (screenPosition < gameRef.size.x - width/2) {
        position.x = screenPosition;
      }
      print('Reset Key to false');
      rightPressed = false;
    }
  }
}

class Square extends SpriteComponent
    with HasGameRef<GameTemplate>, CollisionCallbacks {

  final spriteVelocity  = 100;
  double screenPosition = 0.0;
  bool isCollision      = false;

  Square(Sprite sprite) {
    debugMode = true;
    this.sprite = sprite;
    size = Vector2(50.0, 50.0);
    position = Vector2(100.0, 100.0);
    add(RectangleHitbox());
  }

  @override
  void update(double dt) {
    super.update(dt);

    // Fall down the screen
    screenPosition = position.y + spriteVelocity * dt ;
    if (screenPosition < gameRef.size.y - height/2){
        position.y = screenPosition;
    } else {
      position.y = 0;
    }

  }
}
```

Discussion

In the example code, collision detection code has been added to indicate when the square and ship sprites intersect. The RectangleHitBox is used to determine when a collision occurs, setting the isCollision flag to true. In the update method, a print statement will then display a message indicating the event has been reported, before resetting the flag to false.

The debugMode property is used to show a friendly guide around our sprite, as seen in Figure 17-5. With this property set to true, you are able to see the positional coordinates of the sprite in use.

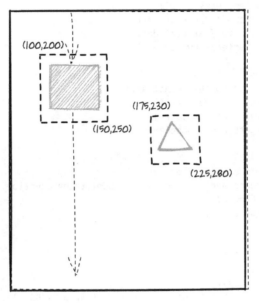

Figure 17-5. Collision detection

A message is displayed when the collision detection is triggered. Collision detection is a useful way to manage interaction between components. Imagine the amount of code you would have to write to manually check if items were intersecting on-screen. From a practical perspective, if you have the opportunity to use collision detection, you should use it.

17.7 Adding Text Rendering

Problem

You want to add text to the on-screen viewport using the Flame game engine.

Solution

Use the TextBoxComponent to render information on the game viewport. The component can use the TextStyle widget, and thus be customized to suit requirements.

Here's an example of how to incorporate the `TextBoxComponent` into your application and write a basic text object on-screen:

```dart
import 'package:flame/collisions.dart';
import 'package:flame/events.dart';
import 'package:flame/flame.dart';
import 'package:flame/game.dart';
import 'package:flame/components.dart';
import 'package:flutter/material.dart';
import 'package:flutter/services.dart';

void main() async {
  WidgetsFlutterBinding.ensureInitialized();
  await Flame.device.setPortrait();
  final shapeGame = GameTemplate();
  runApp(GameWidget(game: shapeGame));
}

class GameTemplate extends FlameGame
    with HasKeyboardHandlerComponents, HasCollisionDetection {
  late Ship shipPlayer;
  late Square squareEnemy;

  @override
  Future<void> onLoad() async {
    super.onLoad();
    add(HeaderTitle());
    add(shipPlayer = Ship(await loadSprite('triangle.png')));
    add(squareEnemy = Square(await loadSprite('square.png')));
  }
}

class Ship extends SpriteComponent
    with HasGameRef<GameTemplate>, CollisionCallbacks {

  final spriteVelocity  = 500;
  double screenPosition = 0.0;
  bool leftPressed      = false;
  bool rightPressed     = false;
  bool isCollision      = false;

  Ship(Sprite sprite) {
    debugMode = true;
    this.sprite = sprite;
    size = Vector2(50.0, 50.0);
    anchor = Anchor.center;
    position = Vector2(200.0, 200.0);
    add(RectangleHitbox());
    add(KeyboardListenerComponent(
        // keyUp: {
        // },
        keyDown: {
```

```dart
            LogicalKeyboardKey.keyA: (keysPressed) { return leftPressed  = true; },
            LogicalKeyboardKey.keyD: (keysPressed) { return rightPressed = true; },
        },
      ),
    );
  }

  @override
  void update(double dt) {
    super.update(dt);

    if (leftPressed == true){
      screenPosition = position.x - spriteVelocity * dt ;
      if (screenPosition > 0 + width/2){
        position.x = screenPosition;
      }
      print('Reset Key to false');
      leftPressed = false;
    }
    if (rightPressed == true){
      screenPosition = position.x + spriteVelocity * dt;
      if (screenPosition < gameRef.size.x - width/2) {
        position.x = screenPosition;
      }
      print('Reset Key to false');
      rightPressed = false;
    }
  }
}

class Square extends SpriteComponent
    with HasGameRef<GameTemplate>, CollisionCallbacks {

  final spriteVelocity  = 100;
  double screenPosition = 0.0;
  bool isCollision      = false;

  Square(Sprite sprite) {
    debugMode = true;
    this.sprite = sprite;
    size = Vector2(50.0, 50.0);
    position = Vector2(100.0, 100.0);
    add(RectangleHitbox());
  }

  @override
  void onCollision(Set<Vector2> intersectionPoints, PositionComponent other) {
    super.onCollision(intersectionPoints, other);
    isCollision = true;
  }

  @override
```

```
    void update(double dt) {
      super.update(dt);

      // Fall down the screen
      screenPosition = position.y + spriteVelocity * dt ;
      if (screenPosition < gameRef.size.y - height/2){
          position.y = screenPosition;
      } else {
        position.y = 0.0;
      }

      if (isCollision){
        print('Collision!');
        isCollision = false;
      }
    }
  }
}


class HeaderTitle extends TextBoxComponent {

  final textPaint = TextPaint(
      style: const TextStyle(
          color: Colors.white,
          fontSize: 22.0,
          fontFamily: 'Awesome Font'));

  HeaderTitle(){
    position = Vector2(100.0, 20.0);
  }

  @override
  Future<void> onLoad() async {
    super.onLoad();
  }

  @override
  void render(Canvas c) {
    textPaint.render(c, "MyAwesome Game", position);
  }
}
```

Discussion

In the example code, text is rendered to the screen using the `textPaint.render`
method. Text position is set to the top of the screen using a `Vector2` structure denot-
ing the x- and y-axes.

As shown in Figure 17-6, the text "Space Square Attack" is displayed on the screen
when the application is run. Coordinates for the placement of the text are defined in
the `onLoad` method and use the screen dimensions. The color of the text to be

displayed is defined with the TextPaint method that also defines the font to be used on-screen. The textPaint.render method requires a canvas object, the text to be displayed, and an on-screen *x, y* coordinate specifying the position of the text.

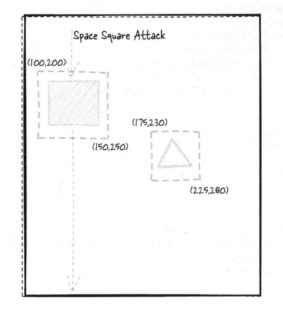

Figure 17-6. Text rendering

Styling uses the same mechanism as Flutter; therefore, you should be able to get the aesthetic desired. If you wish to use a custom font (reference Recipes 8.4 and 10.1), this will need to be added to the *pubspec.yaml* prior to it being made available for use in the application.

17.8 Adding Graphic Primitives

Problem

You want to draw basic shapes as part of your game application using Flame and Flutter.

Solution

Use the Flame game engine to access Canvas objects for rendering graphic primitives such as rectangles, circles, and lines. Flame includes the Flutter Canvas object, so it is able to use the existing API to generate shapes.

Here's an example of an application demonstrating how to render basic shapes using the Flame game engine:

```dart
import 'dart:io';
import 'dart:math';

import 'package:flame/collisions.dart';
import 'package:flame/events.dart';
import 'package:flame/flame.dart';
import 'package:flame/game.dart';
import 'package:flame/components.dart';
import 'package:flutter/material.dart';
import 'package:flutter/services.dart';
import 'package:flame_audio/flame_audio.dart';


void main() async {
  WidgetsFlutterBinding.ensureInitialized();
  await Flame.device.setPortrait();
  final shapeGame = GameTemplate();
  runApp(GameWidget(game: shapeGame));
}

class GameTemplate extends FlameGame
    with HasKeyboardHandlerComponents, HasCollisionDetection {
  late Ship shipPlayer;
  late Square squareEnemy;

  @override
  Future<void> onLoad() async {
    super.onLoad();
    add(HeaderTitle());
    add(RectComponent(size.x, size.y));
    add(shipPlayer = Ship(await loadSprite('triangle.png')));
    add(squareEnemy = Square(await loadSprite('square.png')));
  }
}

class Ship extends SpriteComponent
    with HasGameRef<GameTemplate>, CollisionCallbacks {

  final spriteVelocity  = 500;
  double screenPosition = 0.0;
  bool leftPressed      = false;
  bool rightPressed     = false;
  bool isCollision      = false;

  Ship(Sprite sprite) {
    debugMode = true;
    this.sprite = sprite;
    size = Vector2(50.0, 50.0);
    anchor = Anchor.center;
    position = Vector2(200.0, 200.0);
    add(RectangleHitbox());
    add(KeyboardListenerComponent(
```

```dart
      // keyUp: {
      // },
      keyDown: {
        LogicalKeyboardKey.keyA: (keysPressed) { return leftPressed  = true; },
        LogicalKeyboardKey.keyD: (keysPressed) { return rightPressed = true; },
      },
    ),
  );
}

@override
void update(double dt) {
  super.update(dt);

  if (leftPressed == true){
    screenPosition = position.x - spriteVelocity * dt ;
    if (screenPosition > 0 + width/2){
      position.x = screenPosition;
    }
    print('Reset Key to false');
    leftPressed = false;
  }
  if (rightPressed == true){
    screenPosition = position.x + spriteVelocity * dt;
    if (screenPosition < gameRef.size.x - width/2) {
      position.x = screenPosition;
    }
    print('Reset Key to false');
    rightPressed = false;
  }
}
}

class Square extends SpriteComponent
    with HasGameRef<GameTemplate>, CollisionCallbacks {

  final spriteVelocity  = 100;
  double screenPosition = 0.0;
  bool isCollision      = false;

  Square(Sprite sprite) {
    debugMode = true;
    this.sprite = sprite;
    size = Vector2(50.0, 50.0);
    position = Vector2(100.0, 100.0);
    add(RectangleHitbox());
  }

  @override
  void onCollision(Set<Vector2> intersectionPoints, PositionComponent other) {
    super.onCollision(intersectionPoints, other);
      isCollision = true;
```

```
    }

    @override
    void update(double dt) {
      super.update(dt);

      // Fall down the screen
      screenPosition = position.y + spriteVelocity * dt ;
      if (screenPosition < gameRef.size.y - height/2){
          position.y = screenPosition;
      } else {
        position.y = 0.0;
      }

      if (isCollision){
        print('Collision!');
        isCollision = false;
      }
    }
  }
}

class HeaderTitle extends TextBoxComponent {

  final double xHeaderPosition = 100.0;
  final double yHeaderPosition = 20.0;

  final textPaint = TextPaint(
      style: const TextStyle(
          color: Colors.white,
          fontSize: 22.0,
          fontFamily: 'Awesome Font'));

  HeaderTitle(){
    position = Vector2(xHeaderPosition, yHeaderPosition);
  }

  @override
  Future<void> onLoad() async {
    super.onLoad();
  }

  @override
  void render(Canvas c) {
    textPaint.render(c, "Super Square Attack", position);
  }
}

// Add a [Color] Rect on screen
class RectComponent extends Component {
  double xComponentPosition = 0;
  double yComponentPosition = 0;
  static double xRectWidth  = 50;
```

```
static double yRectHeight = 50;
final spriteVelocity    = 100;
Vector2 size            = Vector2(0.0, 0.0);
double screenPosition   = 0.0;
bool isCollision        = false;
var seed                = Random().nextDouble();

final paint = Paint()
  ..color = Colors.white
  ..strokeWidth = 4;

RectComponent(x, y) {
  size.x = x;
  size.y = y;
  var seed          = Random().nextDouble();
  // xComponentPosition = x/2;
  xComponentPosition = randomHorizontalPosition(size.x - xRectWidth/2);
  yComponentPosition = y/2;
}

double randomHorizontalPosition(double x){
  var seed          = Random().nextDouble();
  return (seed * (size.x - 0.0) + 0.0);
}

@override
void update(double dt) {
  super.update(dt);

  // Fall down the screen
  screenPosition = yComponentPosition + spriteVelocity * dt ;
  if (screenPosition < size.y - yRectHeight/2){
    yComponentPosition = screenPosition;
  } else {
    // Random spawn at new X location
    xComponentPosition = randomHorizontalPosition(size.x - xRectWidth/2);
    yComponentPosition = 0.0;
  }
}

@override
void render(Canvas canvas) {
  super.render(canvas);

  // xStartPos, aayStartPos, xRectWidth, yRectHeight
  canvas.drawRect(
      Rect.fromLTWH(
        xComponentPosition,
        yComponentPosition,
        xRectWidth,
        yRectHeight
      ),
```

```
        paint);
    }
}
```

Discussion

In the example, the Canvas class is used to draw a rectangle on-screen. Canvas is not specific to the Flame game engine and can be used directly in Flutter. The Flame game engine includes the Canvas graphic primitives, making object rendering similar to many other languages, e.g., JavaScript.

A rectangle is applied to the screen and slowly moves vertically, as shown in Figure 17-7. Using the Flame Component class, each graphic primitive can control its own properties and lifecycle. Primitives for Rect, Line, and Circle are among the options available to developers.

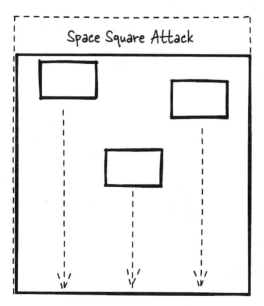

Figure 17-7. Rectangle graphic primitive

Each primitive inherits from the base class, meaning methods such as update and render are available to use. The Rect primitive includes the update and render methods used to control the information displayed on-screen. To draw a line, four points are required that use the Offset object to hold the coordinates. As the update function is not used in this instance, we do not need to declare it. The Circle class again inherits from the Flame Component class. Render is used to call the canvas.draw Circle method with a single offset point, radius, and paint object. The method uses the radius value to define the dimension of the circle to be displayed.

17.9 Adding Sound Effects

Problem

You want to add audio to be played in a game developed with Flame and Flutter.

Solution

Use the *flame_audio* package to provide in-game audio capable of playing both music and samples. The package includes a caching option to minimize time taken to load music and background samples.

Here's an example of an application that demonstrates how to add and play an audio file using the Flame game engine:

```dart
import 'dart:io';
import 'dart:math';

import 'package:flame/collisions.dart';
import 'package:flame/events.dart';
import 'package:flame/flame.dart';
import 'package:flame/game.dart';
import 'package:flame/components.dart';
import 'package:flutter/material.dart';
import 'package:flutter/services.dart';
import 'package:flame_audio/flame_audio.dart';


void main() async {
  WidgetsFlutterBinding.ensureInitialized();
  await Flame.device.setPortrait();
  final shapeGame = GameTemplate();
  runApp(GameWidget(game: shapeGame));
}

class GameTemplate extends FlameGame
    with HasKeyboardHandlerComponents, HasCollisionDetection {
  late Ship shipPlayer;
  late Square squareEnemy;
  late PowerUp powerUp;

  @override
  Future<void> onLoad() async {
    super.onLoad();
    add(HeaderTitle());
    add(RectComponent(size.x, size.y));
    add(shipPlayer = Ship(await loadSprite('triangle.png')));
    add(powerUp = PowerUp(await loadSprite('powerup.png')));
    add(squareEnemy = Square(await loadSprite('square.png')));
  }
}
```

```dart
class Ship extends SpriteComponent
    with HasGameRef<GameTemplate>, CollisionCallbacks {

  final spriteVelocity  = 500;
  double screenPosition = 0.0;
  bool leftPressed      = false;
  bool rightPressed     = false;
  bool isCollision      = false;

  Ship(Sprite sprite) {
    debugMode = true;
    this.sprite = sprite;
    size = Vector2(50.0, 50.0);
    anchor = Anchor.center;
    position = Vector2(200.0, 200.0);
    add(RectangleHitbox());
    add(KeyboardListenerComponent(
        // keyUp: {
        // },
        keyDown: {
          LogicalKeyboardKey.keyA: (keysPressed) { return leftPressed  = true; },
          LogicalKeyboardKey.keyD: (keysPressed) { return rightPressed = true; },
        },
      ),
    );
  }

  @override
  void update(double dt) {
    super.update(dt);

    if (leftPressed == true){
      screenPosition = position.x - spriteVelocity * dt ;
      if (screenPosition > 0 + width/2){
        position.x = screenPosition;
      }
      print('Reset Key to false');
      leftPressed = false;
    }
    if (rightPressed == true){
      screenPosition = position.x + spriteVelocity * dt;
      if (screenPosition < gameRef.size.x - width/2) {
        position.x = screenPosition;
      }
      print('Reset Key to false');
      rightPressed = false;
    }
  }
}

class Square extends SpriteComponent
```

```
    with HasGameRef<GameTemplate>, CollisionCallbacks {

  final spriteVelocity  = 100;
  double screenPosition = 0.0;
  bool isCollision       = false;

  Square(Sprite sprite) {
    debugMode = true;
    this.sprite = sprite;
    size = Vector2(50.0, 50.0);
    position = Vector2(100.0, 100.0);
    add(RectangleHitbox());
  }

  @override
  void onCollision(Set<Vector2> intersectionPoints, PositionComponent other) {
    super.onCollision(intersectionPoints, other);
      isCollision = true;
  }

  @override
  void update(double dt) {
    super.update(dt);

    // Fall down the screen
    screenPosition = position.y + spriteVelocity * dt ;
    if (screenPosition < gameRef.size.y - height/2){
        position.y = screenPosition;
    } else {
      position.y = 0.0;
    }

    if (isCollision){
      print('Collision!');
      isCollision = false;
    }
  }
}


class PowerUp extends SpriteComponent
    with HasGameRef<GameTemplate>, CollisionCallbacks {

  final spriteVelocity  = 100;
  final soundDelay       = 1000;
  var duration = const Duration(seconds: 1);
  double screenPosition = 0.0;
  bool isCollision       = false;
  bool isPlaying         = false;

  PowerUp(Sprite sprite) {
    // debugMode = true;
```

```dart
    this.sprite = sprite;
    size = Vector2(50.0, 50.0);
    position = Vector2(400.0, 100.0);
    add(RectangleHitbox());
  }

  @override
  void onCollision(Set<Vector2> intersectionPoints, PositionComponent other) {
    super.onCollision(intersectionPoints, other);
    isCollision = true;
    if (isPlaying == false) {
      isPlaying = true;
      playSound();
    }
    // isPlaying    = true;
  }

  @override
  Future<void> onLoad() async {
    super.onLoad();
    await FlameAudio.audioCache.load('powerup.wav');
  }

  void playSound() async {
    await FlameAudio.play('powerup.wav');
  }

  @override
  void update(double dt) {
    super.update(dt);

    print (screenPosition);

    // Fall down the screen
    screenPosition = position.y + spriteVelocity * dt ;
    if (screenPosition < gameRef.size.y - height/2){
      position.y = screenPosition;
    } else {
      isPlaying = false;
      position.y = 0.0;
    }

    if (isCollision){
      isCollision = false;
    }
  }
}

class HeaderTitle extends TextBoxComponent {

  final double xHeaderPosition = 100.0;
  final double yHeaderPosition = 20.0;
```

```dart
      final textPaint = TextPaint(
          style: const TextStyle(
              color: Colors.white,
              fontSize: 22.0,
              fontFamily: 'Awesome Font'));

      HeaderTitle(){
        position = Vector2(xHeaderPosition, yHeaderPosition);
      }

      @override
      Future<void> onLoad() async {
        super.onLoad();
      }

      @override
      void render(Canvas c) {
        textPaint.render(c, "Super Square Attack", position);
      }
}

// Add a [Color] Rect on screen
class RectComponent extends Component {
    double xComponentPosition = 0;
    double yComponentPosition = 0;
    static double xRectWidth  = 50;
    static double yRectHeight = 50;
    final spriteVelocity       = 100;
    Vector2 size               = Vector2(0.0, 0.0);
    double screenPosition      = 0.0;
    bool isCollision           = false;
    var seed                   = Random().nextDouble();

    final paint = Paint()
      ..color = Colors.white
      ..strokeWidth = 4;

    RectComponent(x, y) {
      size.x = x;
      size.y = y;
      var seed           = Random().nextDouble();
      // xComponentPosition = x/2;
      xComponentPosition = randomHorizontalPosition(size.x - xRectWidth/2);
      yComponentPosition = y/2;
    }

    double randomHorizontalPosition(double x){
      var seed           = Random().nextDouble();
      return (seed * (size.x - 0.0) + 0.0);
    }
```

```
@override
void update(double dt) {
  super.update(dt);

  // Fall down the screen
  screenPosition = yComponentPosition + spriteVelocity * dt ;
  if (screenPosition < size.y - yRectHeight/2){
    yComponentPosition = screenPosition;
  } else {
    // Random spawn at new X location
    xComponentPosition = randomHorizontalPosition(size.x - xRectWidth/2);
    yComponentPosition = 0.0;
  }
}

@override
void render(Canvas canvas) {
  super.render(canvas);

  // xStartPos, aayStartPos, xRectWidth, yRectHeight
  canvas.drawRect(
      Rect.fromLTWH(
        xComponentPosition,
        yComponentPosition,
        xRectWidth,
        yRectHeight
      ),
      paint);
  }
}
```

Discussion

In the example code, a WAV audio file is used to indicate that the on-screen sprite component has experienced a collision. Each time the sprite comes into contact with the square component, a collision will have occurred.

When a collision is detected between the player and the power-up sprite, a sound is played to indicate this event has occurred, as shown in Figure 17-8.

Adding audio requires the installation of the *flame_audio* Flutter package. Loading the audio is an asynchronous activity, so it should be performed in the onLoad method. In the example, the audio is cached, and as there is only one file, it uses the load method. If you have multiple audio files, consider using the loadAll method, which takes an array of sound files.

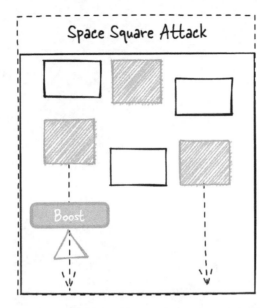

Figure 17-8. Associating a sound effect with a sprite

Organize the assets folder to incorporate the sound file. Assets should be added to a subfolder for ease of access within the application. In the example, the folder *assets/audio* is used to hold the related sound file.

When playing the audio sample, avoid adding it to the update loop unless it needs to be frequently called. Typically, you will want to set a flag to indicate that the sound is playing and then have a duration or event reset the flag. Taking this approach means your code is less prone to overlapping sound effects, which can happen with long clips or tight inner game loops.

Sound effects require the application to work in cooperation with the device lifecycle. For web and desktop devices, this is not too problematic. If you are targeting a mobile device, you will need to ensure your application respects whether the application is in the foreground or background. Specifically, the onPaused and onResumed methods will need to be invoked to react to system changes, such as an application being run in the background.

Setting Up Your Environment

Dart is a feature-rich language that provides variables, data handling, control flow, and much more. Experience with languages such as JavaScript, Python, and C will mean your transition to Dart should not be difficult. If you are new to programming, I believe you will be pleasantly surprised by how quickly you can produce an application.

The Dart and Flutter teams have provided a comprehensive treasure trove of tutorials. Even better, the community working in these technologies has raised the bar for immersive solutions and demonstrations to quickly get you up to speed.

In this appendix, you will learn how to install the Dart software development kit (SDK). Multiple options exist to run a Dart environment, so I will walk you through the most common options (e.g., DartPad, Android Studio, and VS Code).

Determining Which Dart Installation to Use

Dart can be used directly from the browser in a predefined environment such as DartPad (*https://dartpad.dev*).

Using DartPad in the browser will be sufficient for starting out and trying the language. If you intend to build a modest application and do not require external dependencies (e.g., graphics, files, etc.), the browser environment will align with your use case. Once you are ready for a more complex scenario than using shared SDK-provided libraries available in DartPad, you will want to explore other development options.

Alternatively, if you have the hardware to support it, the Dart SDK can be installed locally on your device. In this instance, there are a number of steps to fulfill prior to being able to start developing with Dart. If you already have an IDE environment such as VS Code or Android Studio, you can use a plug-in to add support for Dart/Flutter development.

Over the course of this appendix, the main options for development are discussed in further detail to get you started. Personal preference will play a major part in the choice of installation followed.

Running Dart in DartPad

Dart provides an online environment to test and run code. DartPad is an excellent online editor that can be used through a browser to develop and test your code. By using DartPad, you can quickly develop code and share it with a selected audience, e.g., *dart.dev* or *flutter.dev* using a Git repository. Go to DartPad (*https://dartpad.dev*) and start to enter your code there.

DartPad is a really powerful tool that you should consider irrespective of which type of installation you have selected. Figure A-1 shows how a simple "Hello, World!" application would look in the DartPad interface.

Figure A-1. The DartPad interface

Starting DartPad presents a new instance ready to develop. The interface presents a simple editor environment with a code editor, a console, and documentation windows. The code editor on the left-hand side enables you to start coding in an intelligent window. The editor constantly provides feedback on helpful information for you to develop your code.

Once your code is ready to run, the output will be displayed in the console window. In the preceding example, our program output is shown. Note: DartPad also works with Flutter applications, so you get the best of both worlds.

Another helpful feature is that there are a number of predefined sample applications available that cover both Dart and Flutter. If you want to try the Dart language, you will find that the samples will quickly demonstrate a variety of use cases. The typical use case for DartPad is to quickly write small sections of code that can be publicly shared using GitHub gists. When using this approach, the rendered output can then be accessed via a unique URL associated with the gist.

If you are not familiar with gists, they are snippets of code that are linked to your GitHub account. Sign into your GitHub account and then go to GitHub Gist (*http:// gist.github.com*). From there you can paste your code snippet and share it either publicly or as a secret (only available to those with the associated URL).

Installing the Flutter Framework

Installing the Flutter framework involves a series of steps that depend on your operating system. To get the latest guidance, visit the Flutter install web page (*https:// oreil.ly/4WHvH*). When you install the Flutter framework, you also get the Dart SDK installation added to your development environment. Once you have Flutter installed, use Flutter Doctor to verify the installation has completed successfully.

Using Flutter Doctor

Setting up Dart and Flutter is a multistep process. To assist with the correct installation steps for your preferred operating system, use the `flutter doctor` tool to help configure your environment:

```
flutter doctor
```

Depending on your operating system, you will see an output similar to the following:

```
Doctor summary (to see all details, run flutter doctor -v):
[✓] Flutter (Channel stable, 3.3.3, on Ubuntu 20.04.5 LTS 5.15.0-48-generic,
    locale en_GB.UTF-8)
[✓] Android toolchain - develop for Android devices (Android SDK version 33.0.0)
[✓] Chrome - develop for the web
[✓] Linux toolchain - develop for Linux desktop
[✓] Android Studio (version 2021.3)
[✓] Android Studio (version 2021.2)
[✓] Connected device (2 available)
[✓] HTTP Host Availability

• No issues found!
```

The preceding command will output the configuration associated with your machine. Use this to diagnose the current state and whether any changes need to be made. A key thing to remember when installing both Flutter and Dart is the respective locations of the framework and SDK on your development machine. If you use Android Studio, you may need to provide this information when cloning repositories. In this situation, use `flutter doctor` with the verbose option to see the configuration on your machine, including the path to Flutter SDK:

```
flutter doctor -v
```

Based on your operating system, you will see a more in-depth analysis of your current configuration, as shown in the following:

```
[✓] Flutter (Channel stable, 3.3.3, on Ubuntu 20.04.5 LTS 5.15.0-48-generic,
    locale en_GB.UTF-8)
    • Flutter version 3.3.3 on channel stable at
      /home/rosera/snap/flutter/common/flutter
    • Upstream repository https://github.com/flutter/flutter.git
    • Framework revision 18a827f393 (10 days ago), 2022-09-28 10:03:14 -0700
    • Engine revision 5c984c26eb
    • Dart version 2.18.2
    • DevTools version 2.15.0

[✓] Android toolchain - develop for Android devices (Android SDK version 33.0.0)
    • Android SDK at /home/rosera/Android/Sdk
    • Platform android-33, build-tools 33.0.0
    • Java binary at: /snap/android-studio/124/android-studio/jre/bin/java
    • Java version OpenJDK Runtime Environment (build 11.0.13+0-b1751.21-8125866)
    • All Android licenses accepted.

[✓] Chrome - develop for the web
    • Chrome at google-chrome

[✓] Linux toolchain - develop for Linux desktop
    • clang version 6.0.0-1ubuntu2 (tags/RELEASE_600/final)
    • cmake version 3.10.2
    • ninja version 1.8.2
    • pkg-config version 0.29.1

[✓] Android Studio (version 2021.3)
    • Android Studio at /snap/android-studio/124/android-studio
    • Flutter plugin version 70.2.3
    • Dart plugin version 213.7433
    • Java version OpenJDK Runtime Environment (build 11.0.13+0-b1751.21-8125866)

[✓] Android Studio (version 2021.2)
    • Android Studio at /snap/android-studio/123/android-studio
    • Flutter plugin version 70.0.2
    • Dart plugin version 212.5744
    • Java version OpenJDK Runtime Environment (build 11.0.12+0-b1504.28-7817840)
```

```
[✓] Connected device (2 available)
    • Linux (desktop) • linux  • linux-x64
    • Ubuntu 20.04.5 LTS 5.15.0-48-generic
    • Chrome (web)    • chrome • web-javascript • Google Chrome 105.0.5195.125

[✓] HTTP Host Availability
    • All required HTTP hosts are available

• No issues found!
```

Alternatively, you can use the very verbose option, `flutter doctor -vv`, for an extremely detailed view of the current installation.

In addition to the preceding, you may wish to use `flutter doctor` to perform the license agreement necessary to work with Android:

```
flutter doctor --android-licenses
```

The output should be similar to the following:

```
All SDK package licenses accepted.======] 100% Computing updates...
```

Installing the Dart SDK

If you wish to only use Dart, follow the installation instructions at Get the Dart SDK (*https://dart.dev/get-dart*). The SDK supports Linux (e.g., Debian and Ubuntu), macOS, and Windows platforms. Up-to-date instructions on the installation of the Dart SDK are available via the dart.dev site (*https://dart.dev/get-dart*).

Performing an SDK installation directly to the operating system means the SDK can be made accessible from any software running on your device.

Developing with VS Code

To use VS Code, you have to install the SDK first (see previous section). If you choose to work in this environment, updating the editor to support Dart/Flutter is just a case of adding the relevant extension. Instructions for VS Code are documented at the Flutter Visual Studio Code web page (*https://oreil.ly/2Xsis*). From within the editor, select the extension icon and search for Flutter. Click the install icon to add both Flutter and Dart functionality.

If you are coming from a web development background, you will likely be familiar with VS Code and therefore it may seem like a good fit. VS Code provides a low barrier to entry when working with Dart/Flutter. The maintainers of this extension assume you will want both Dart and Flutter, so the installation process invokes both.

Once the extensions are installed, you will be able to create a Dart application within the environment. At this point, there will be some additional elements added to the user interface, specifically the ability to run Dart directly from within the editor. In addition, VS Code will show information based on the user context. When code is being developed, the IDE will check on the validity of that code automatically. The code editor will also render run/debug icons dynamically when code compiles without errors. When you graduate to using Flutter, VS Code will seek to target a particular device (e.g., web, Android, iOS, etc.) based on your operating system setup.

If you are already working within this environment, it will be a no-brainer to add this extension. In terms of updates, the environment will automatically indicate when a new version is available and allow the update to take place.

To uninstall the extension, you would select the plug-in from the extension menu and then choose the uninstall option.

Extending Android Studio to Support Dart

Ensure you have the Flutter framework installed first. To use Android Studio, you can simply select the Flutter or Dart plug-in. Doing this will add the desired functionality to the development environment. Once selected, Android Studio will then go about automatically configuring your environment with defaults to use the necessary plug-in.

If you are coming from an Android or Java development background, you will more than likely be familiar with Android Studio or IntelliJ. The main use case for this editor is developing Android-based applications. Adding support for Flutter and Dart is relatively easy via the application interface. Instructions for Android Studio are documented at the Flutter Android Studio and IntelliJ web page (*https://oreil.ly/TzUir*).

Despite the name, Android Studio can actually work with other languages. The process of adding Flutter is available at the click of a button and is fully integrated into the environment.

Once installed, Dart/Flutter applications can be selected as the target platform from project initiation. To get started, Android Studio will offer access to Flutter templates as part of the user interface.

Selecting a Release Channel

Release channels provide a mechanism to build code against a specific version of the Dart SDK. The channels are:

Channel	Description
Stable	This channel is meant for production and is updated on a quarterly basis.
Beta	This channel is meant for working with leading-edge updates on a monthly basis.
Dev	This channel is meant for bleeding edge, with updates on a weekly basis.

Based on the preceding, I would suggest that you should be on the stable channel for the majority of use cases. Unless you have a very good reason to use another release channel (e.g., using functionality in the dev/beta channel), stable should be where you do the majority of your development.

Using Flutter Config to Set the Target Platform

Flutter will attempt to create a variety of target platforms by default. Use the "flutter config" command to configure the development environment as required. If you wish to keep the deployment simple, you can tell Flutter to only create a specific target platform.

In the example below, the configuration settings are set to false, meaning the target platform will not be created for new applications:

```
flutter config --no-enable-macos-desktop --no-enable-fuchsia
    --no-enable-windows-desktop --no-enable-ios --no-enable-android
```

The settings for flutter config support a true/false flag, meaning it is relatively straightforward to amend via the command line. With the above command, the creation of a Flutter codebase will only create a web- and Linux-based application.

Configuration supports the target platforms available with Flutter:

Flag	Description
--[no-]enable-web	Enable or disable Flutter for the web. This setting will take effect on the master, beta, and stable channels.
--[no-]enable-linux-desktop	Enable or disable support for desktop on Linux. This setting will take effect on the master, beta, and stable channels.
--[no-]enable-macos-desktop	Enable or disable support for desktop on macOS. This setting will take effect on the master, beta, and stable channels.
--[no-]enable-windows-desktop	Enable or disable support for desktop on Windows. This setting will take effect on the master, beta, and stable channels.
--[no-]enable-android	Enable or disable Flutter for Android. This setting will take effect on the master, beta, and stable channels.
--[no-]enable-ios	Enable or disable Flutter for iOS. This setting will take effect on the master, beta, and stable channels.
--[no-]enable-fuchsia	Enable or disable Flutter for Fuchsia. This setting will take effect on the master channel.

If you want to return to the default configuration, you can reset the environment in the following way:

```
flutter config --clear-features
```

Index

test pyramid, 53
troubleshooting with, 197
user interface testing, 53, 191-198
widgets, automated, 191-194
testWidget, 193
text
find methods and testing, 193
Google Fonts, 80, 115-117
media queries, 118
multiline, 6
Placeholder widget, 121-123
rich text, 117
tabs, 166
text rendering in games, 255-259
theme, 117
vertical lists, 134
Text widget
creating, 84, 86-88
Google Fonts with, 117
SliverList widget and, 144
vertical lists, 134
TextBoxComponent, 255-259
textPaint.render, 258
textScaleFactor, 129
TextStyle widget, 255
theme
setting text, 117
tabs, 166
ThemeData settings, 166
this keyword
converting JSON data to Dart classes, 180
omission of, 42, 44
timeouts, integration tests, 196
Title property, 96
titles
AppBar header, 95-96
drawers, 163
true keyword, 5
try block, 19, 20
type checking, VS Code, 278
type safety, 1, 9

U

Uniform Resource Identifier (URI), loading
remote data, 190
Unique key option, 172
unit tests, 53
grouping multiple, 58-61
versus integration tests, 58

running, 56-61
in test pyramid, 53
versus widget tests, 193
update method (Flame), 248, 264
user interface, 115-129
(see also navigation)
Google Fonts package, using, 115-117
identifying host platform, 119
LayoutBuilder widget, 123-126
media queries, 126-129
Placeholder widget, 121-123
rich text, 117
setting theme, 117
testing, 53, 191
widget tree, 71-73
UTF-16 coding, 6

V

Value key option, 172
values, 3
(see also keys/values)
assigning to variables, 3
conditional actions, 16-18
dynamic values and Maps, 34
enum, 18
null values, 4, 8, 24
optional parameters, 23
returning from functions, 25
stateful widgets and, 85-88
variables
$ (dollar sign) for in print statements, 7, 37
adding constant variables at runtime, 8
anonymous functions, 26
assigning values to, 3
Boolean, 4
data types, 1-9
declaring, 3
double values, 4
immutability of, 1
integer values, 3
labels, 3
naming, 3
nullable, 4, 8, 24
private, 87
string, 5
test construction and, 57
using, 1-9
Vector2, 245, 258
vertical lists, 131-134

viewport
    Container widget, 98
    Expanded widget, 111-114
    game, 243
    horizontal lists and, 135-137
    thresholds, 126
VS Code
    creating sample test package, 56
    Dart setup, 2, 277

W

while loop, 13-15
whitespace, 99, 101-103
widget tree, 71-73, 91, 128
widgets, 71, 83-114
    as composable, 71
    creating stateful, 85-88
    creating stateless, 83-85
    importance of, 83
    passing information between with keys,
        170-172
    refactoring, 83, 88-91
    rendering performance, 72
    stateful versus stateless, 65

testing, automated, 191-194
    understanding, 70-73
    wireframes, 66
WidgetTester, 193
width
    columns, 107
    Container widget, 97-98
    media queries, 128
    Placeholder widget, 123
    SizedBox widget, 101-103, 107
wireframes, 65
with keyword, 51
wrapping and GridView widget, 145

X

XCTest, 197

Y

YAML/Yet Another Markup Language, 77, 81
    (see also pubspec.yaml file)

Z

z-order, 246

About the Author

Rich loves building things in the cloud and tinkering with different technologies. Lately this involves either Kubernetes or serverless. Based in the UK, he enjoys attending (ya remember that!) technical conferences and speaking to other people about new technologies. When he's not working, he likes spending time with his family, playing the guitar, and riding his mountain bike. To improve his development skills, he has also started writing smaller utility applications to simplify the more repetitive tasks (e.g., image manipulation, text manipulation, studying for certifications). Rich is also the author of *Hands-On Serverless Computing with Google Cloud* (Packt Publishing, 2020).

Colophon

The animal on the cover of *Flutter and Dart Cookbook* is a great peacock moth (*Saturni pyri*). It is known by several names, including giant peacock moth, giant emperor moth, and Viennese emperor moth.

Great peacock moths have a wingspan of 15 to 20 centimeters. Their bodies are chocolaty brown, and their wings have ocellar spots at the center of each wing surrounded by black, brown, and grey concentric circles, which stand out on the greyish-brown background color of the wing. At night, these spots look like the eyes of nocturnal birds of prey and thus function as a way to scare off potential predators.

The ideal habitat for these moths is a dry, hot, open landscape with trees and shrubs. They feed on tree and plant sugars, preferring walnut trees in the wild and ashes and stone fruit trees in captivity. They can be found in an expansive region that includes southern Europe, northern Africa, and parts of the Middle East.

Great peacock moths are not endangered; however, many of the animals on O'Reilly covers are endangered. All of them are important to the world.

The cover illustration is by Karen Montgomery, based on an antique line engraving from *Histoire Naturelle*. The cover fonts are Gilroy Semibold and Guardian Sans. The text font is Adobe Minion Pro; the heading font is Adobe Myriad Condensed; and the code font is Dalton Maag's Ubuntu Mono.

Printed in the USA
CPSIA information can be obtained
at www.ICGtesting.com
JSHW051344041223
53222JS00012B/132

9 781098 119515